THE PACIFIC CREST TRAIL

By William R. Gray   *Photographed by Sam Abell*

Prepared by the Special Publications Division
National Geographic Society, Washington, D.C.

THE PACIFIC CREST TRAIL

By WILLIAM R. GRAY
National Geographic Staff
Photographed by SAM ABELL

Published by
THE NATIONAL GEOGRAPHIC SOCIETY
MELVIN M. PAYNE, *President*
MELVILLE BELL GROSVENOR, *Editor-in-Chief*
GILBERT M. GROSVENOR, *Editor*

Prepared by
THE SPECIAL PUBLICATIONS DIVISION
ROBERT L. BREEDEN, *Editor*
DONALD J. CRUMP, *Associate Editor*
PHILIP B. SILCOTT, *Senior Editor*
MERRILL WINDSOR, *Managing Editor*
LINDA M. BRIDGE, BARBARA GRAZZINI, *Research*

Illustrations
DAVID R. BRIDGE, *Picture Editor*
ABIGAIL T. BRETT, SUSAN C. BURNS, JAN NAGEL
    CLARKSON, RONALD M. FISHER, MARGARET
    MCKELWAY JOHNSON, TOM MELHAM, *Picture Legends*
GEORGE FOUNDS, *Drawings*

Design and Art Direction
JOSEPH A. TANEY, *Staff Art Director*
JOSEPHINE B. BOLT, *Art Director*
URSULA PERRIN, *Assistant Art Director*
JANE D'ALELIO, *Design Assistant*
JOHN D. GARST, JR., ISKANDAR BADAY, MARGARET A.
    DEANE, NANCY SCHWEICKART, ALFRED L. ZEBARTH,
    Map Research, Design, and Production

Production and Printing
ROBERT W. MESSER, *Production Manager*
GEORGE V. WHITE, *Assistant Production Manager*
RAJA D. MURSHED, NANCY W. GLASER, *Production
    Assistants*
JOHN R. METCALFE, *Engraving and Printing*
MARY G. BURNS, JANE H. BUXTON, MARTA ISABEL
    COONS, NATALIE IGLITZ, SUZANNE J. JACOBSON,
    SANDRA LEE MATTHEWS, SELINA PATTON, JOAN
    PERRY, MARILYN L. WILBUR, KAREN G. WILSON,
    Staff Assistants
BARBARA L. KLEIN, GEORGE BURNESTON, *Index*

Library of Congress CIP Data: page 199

*Overleaf: Against a backdrop of the North
Cascades, larch trees turn September gold
in Benson Basin, Washington.
Page 1: Coals glow in a rock fire ring
as new snow dusts a wilderness campsite.*

*Diamond emblem adopted by the
U. S. Forest Service in 1937 still
marks much of the Pacific Crest
Trail. Since 1971 a new shield
(see hard cover) has evoked the
forests and snowcapped peaks
of the scenic mountain pathway.*

FOREWORD

WHEN MY WANDERINGS of the Cascade Range began, back in the 1940's, I was mystified by little green and white, diamond-shaped signs nailed to trees, reading "Pacific Crest Trail System." What was *that?* I hadn't the foggiest notion. Yet I sensed the diamonds marked a different kind of trail from any I had hiked before; there was a thrilling suggestion of the faraway, the excitement of a bold dream.

Eventually I learned the system was still aborning, though much of the trail wasn't actually new. Often the diamonds appeared along high-meadow and low-valley paths that had been made by boots and hooves over the preceding half-century.

But the dream—the imaginative proposal of Californian Clinton C. Clarke —was new; and its power has grown steadily with the years. A decade ago I would often spend a week walking flower-bright ridges or scrambling up ice-sharpened peaks along the Cascade Crest section of the trail, and see nary another soul. To find such solitude there nowadays one must go in spring, when snows are ten feet deep and rivers are raging with meltwater, or in late fall when storms are cold and furious. In the 1960's a feeling grew all across our land that what we call "civilization" had run out of control, that the world was becoming so noisy and garish and nerve-jangling and spirit-smothering as to be downright hazardous to human life. In unprecedented numbers Americans sought the solace and the healing of wildness. Waiting for them was the dream of Clinton Clarke and his compatriots.

Frankly, I much preferred the lonesome old days of the '40's. But precisely because I am, insofar as the wild country is concerned, a conservative if not a ranting reactionary, I was compelled during the 1950's to join the campaign for wilderness preservation. And it was then, while working toward the goal of a North Cascades National Park—at last achieved in 1968—that I grasped the true genius of the Pacific Crest Trail. My efforts as pamphleteer and propagandist taught me how difficult it is to sway minds with reason alone, that great ventures depend for their success on the inspiration of symbols.

Surely there is no grander, more potent symbol in the West than the 2,400-mile path linking the wilderness of public forests and parks in three states. The trail speaks to me, as do the narrative and photographs in this book, of the interrelation—the unity in diversity—of the shining glaciers hanging above the green-gloomy woods of Agnes Creek in Washington, the emerald plain of Jefferson Park in Oregon, the moonlit granite cliffs of Desolation Valley in California. The trail is the symbol of what we have inherited and must labor to save.

Thanks, Mr. Clarke, for the dream and for the symbol.

HARVEY MANNING
Editor, *The Wild Cascades*
Journal of the North Cascades Conservation Council

Chill wind high in the Sierra Nevada buffets cross-country skier Gunnar Vatvedt.

CONTENTS

THE MOUNTAINS'
GOOD TIDINGS
A PROLOGUE

SNOWBOUND PINNACLES of California's Sierra Nevada towered above me, sparkling with the gold of a dawning sun. Gnarled pines, stunted by the harsh growing conditions at 10,500 feet, ringed an indigo lake still half-choked with ice in mid-June. My eyes traced the path as it dodged among house-size granite boulders near the lake. Breathing the fresh cold air, I thought: Surely this is the essence of the Pacific Crest Trail.

Twelve hundred trail miles to the north, in central Oregon, I labored under a broiling August sun to climb a petrified cataract of black, rough-edged lava that once had flowed from the volcanic cone looming ahead. In the midst of a tortured moonscape I realized that this strange place, too, somehow conveyed the trail's essence.

Chill September rains pelted down as I walked on spongy earth among the moldering trunks of fallen trees in northern Washington; a carpet of grass, ferns, mosses, and mushrooms flourished in the rich soil. By this time, I understood: The essence of the Pacific Crest Trail lies in its very diversity.

Threading 2,400 miles among the loftiest bastions of California, Oregon, and Washington, from the Mexican border to the Canadian, the trail stitches across a patchwork of desert and mountain, meadow and forest, lake and glacier, valley and peak. Hiking through this patchwork, sometimes ranging off the trail on either side, I discovered more than topographic diversity; I encountered a remarkable variety of weather, plants, animals, people, and experiences. I kept watch for rattlesnakes in the Mojave Desert; struggled through hip-deep snow to the summit of Mount Whitney; made friends with an old prospector in forty-niner country; studied a great blue heron fishing a river in northern California; stood entranced by the beauty of Crater Lake; watched the elements create clouds in Oregon; slept in an igloo atop Mount Rainier; basked in a hot spring in Washington; and barely escaped the frigid grasp of winter at the edge of Canada.

Sequel to a storm: An evening campfire dries and warms hikers beside Waptus Lake in Washington. Departing rain clouds streak the sky above a conifer forest, one of many kinds of wilderness along the Pacific Crest Trail.

I crossed trails blazed by resolute explorers of the past and came face to face with dilemmas of the present — clear-cut logging, open-pit mining, smog-damaged forests. Along the way I made lasting friendships, renewed a deep respect for nature, and discovered new strengths and weaknesses within myself. At the end, after months of separation from my normal city life, I better understood an observation of historian Roderick Nash: "...it was ultimately civilization that made possible the appreciation of wilderness."

In the early 1930's, Clinton C. Clarke of Pasadena, California, offered to the world his vision of a continuous trail "along the summit divides of the mountain ranges...traversing the best scenic areas and maintaining an absolute wilderness character." The virtue of such a trail, said Clarke, would lie in helping to preserve wild areas and in encouraging people of "our too-artificial civilization" to return to a simpler life and an appreciation of nature and the outdoors.

The U. S. Forest Service and National Park Service both favored the idea, and two trails that had recently been completed were incorporated as the initial links: the 442-mile Oregon Skyline Trail and a 185-mile segment of the John Muir Trail in California. By 1941 the 445-mile Cascade Crest Trail section in Washington was finished.

Meanwhile, a secretary of the Alhambra, California, Young Men's Christian Association volunteered not only to hike the completed sections but also to explore and evaluate the vast distances of trail route that so far existed only on maps. During the summers of 1935 through 1938, Warren L. Rogers carried his logbook more than 2,000 miles, traveling in relays in the company of 40 different YMCA groups. When I talked with him, a vigorous man in his mid-60's, he happily recalled the exploits of those days and concluded with understandable pride, "Today's trail very closely follows the route we blazed with the relays 40 years ago."

With the trail partially built and completely explored, Clinton Clarke formed a coordinating organization called the Pacific Crest Trail System Conference. He served as president and Warren Rogers was executive secretary. "But our early momentum and successes were halted by World War II," Rogers told me, "and at times after that we thought the idea would never really blossom. But Mr. Clarke kept working diligently until his death in 1957."

In the 1960's a rekindled interest in outdoor sports — backpacking in particular — gave new impetus to the Pacific Crest Trail project. A commission of the Bureau of Outdoor Recreation recommended, Congress passed, and President Lyndon B. Johnson signed — on October 2, 1968 — the National Trails System Act. This not only established a general framework for a system of trails but also specifically named the Appalachian and Pacific Crest as the first national scenic trails in the United States.

Today the Pacific Crest is still partly a dream. Of the 2,400-mile total, more than 800 miles of trail has yet to be built, mostly in extreme northern and southern California. Part of the delay lies in obtaining rights-of-way across private land, and part is in financing trail construction. The Forest Service, charged with building and maintaining the trail, is aiming for completion by 1980. Meanwhile it has marked temporary routes that sometimes trace existing trails but usually follow roads.

"I hope to see the entire permanent trail at least cleared of brush by July 4, 1976, our country's bicentennial," Warren Rogers told me. "It would be an appropriate birthday present to the nation." Continuing his long interest, he serves on the Pacific Crest Trail Advisory Council and has established the Pacific Crest Club, "a non-profit service club whose goal it is to weld together all people interested in the trail."

One of the longest and most majestic hiking paths in the world, the Pacific Crest crosses seven national parks, six state parks, 25 national forests, and—within the forests—14 wilderness areas. It penetrates the wild beauty of the granite peaks of the Sierra and the regal cones of the Cascades. It passes over land once hallowed by Indians and later crisscrossed by explorers and settlers. It winds through cathedral-like groves of virgin forest, and through country that once sheltered immense numbers of deer, elk, bears, and mountain lions. Vast tracts of wilderness still enclose parts of the Pacific Crest Trail, and by hiking only a few miles the backpacker can trade the world of freeways and skyscrapers for a realm of solitude and natural splendor. There the needs are the primal ones—food, water, rest—and the rewards are intensely personal: the pride of surmounting a difficult pass, the simple luxury of falling asleep in a silent arena of rocks, trees, and stars.

Because of the scale of the Pacific Crest route and the rugged country it passes through, most people hike it in short takes—over a weekend, or on a backpacking vacation of a week or two—and thus become familiar with a specific, limited section. A few hardy men and women, no more than two score, have traveled the entire trail. At a steady, muscle-taxing, spirit-rending pace of 15 miles a day, every day, it takes more than five months to cover the whole distance. The reasons given for accepting the challenge of long-distance hiking are varied: a love of wilderness, a kinship with nature, a demanding test.

PACIFIC CREST TRAIL

Extending 2,400 miles from Mexico to Canada, the trail follows a rugged highland course along ridges of the Sierra Nevada and part of the Coast Range in California and the Cascade Range in Oregon and Washington. Completed, permanent sections now comprise almost two-thirds of the distance; elsewhere, signs mark temporary routes. In 1968 Congress designated the Pacific Crest and the Appalachian Trail as the beginning of a national scenic trails system.

My own reasons go back to my childhood when family camping trips and mountain climbs sparked an early delight in the out-of-doors that continued to grow through college years, a delight my wife now shares. And for more than a decade I have harbored a desire to hike a long wilderness trail.

My interest in tackling the Pacific Crest Trail coincided with that of photographer Sam Abell, a veteran backpacker and wilderness photographer. With great anticipation we began to plan our trek. We had portions of two hiking seasons—more than seven months—to cover the distance; we decided to spend three summer and fall months in Oregon and Washington, and four spring and summer months in California. Our plan called for hiking most of the completed trail and sampling the temporary sections. A few side trips would take us to points and persons of interest within a few miles of the main route. As it turned out, when we lowered our packs for the last time at the Canadian border, we had hiked nearly two-thirds of the trail, almost 1,600 miles—the distance from New York City to Denver. Along the way I had worn three pairs of soles off my boots.

The period of planning generated excitement that spiraled as Sam and I pored over our maps and guidebooks, worked out menus of freeze-dried foods, and shopped for packs and boots, tent and sleeping bags.

It also began a camaraderie that would grow throughout the trip. We were about the same age—just under 30—and found we'd had many similar experiences while growing up. Our campfire conversations would ramble from sports to architecture, from old recordings to new politics. And after a few days of walking together we began to appreciate the great importance of friendship to long-distance hikers. Besides the safety factor of having a companion, I found that much of my enjoyment of the trail came through sharing the experience with someone else.

Finally, preparations completed, Sam and I hauled our gear to the airport for the flight from Washington, D. C., to Los Angeles, where a friend would drive us to the trail's southern terminus at the Mexican border. As we sped across the country at 500 miles an hour in the spacious comfort of an airliner, I reflected that soon I would provide my own locomotion and that 10 or 12 miles would easily fill an entire day.

As the plane rushed west, I saw the mist-hung ridges of the Appalachian Mountains slip beneath, watched the peaks of the mighty Rockies rise and recede, and gazed with anticipation as the snowy heights of the Pacific Crest soared before me.

"Climb the mountains and get their good tidings," wrote John Muir. With shared eagerness, Sam and I were about to accept his joyous invitation.

Sunlight bathes a grassy hillside in vivid contrast to shadowed crags and a threatening sky as author Will Gray (front) and a companion, Doug Gosling, hike into Goat Lakes Basin in Washington's North Cascades.

ABOVE: MOUNTAIN HEATHER

Roads, austere landscapes, and distinctive plants characterize
much of the southern California portion of the trail. For long
stretches its temporary route follows highways, as in the San
Felipe Valley where a hay truck thunders past Will. A crippled
Joshua tree arches above a burned-over area in the Mojave
Desert. Near Rosamond, a tumbleweed blows in the wind;
weathered wagon parts rest against an old mining-camp building.

Wind-driven snow of a May storm covers conifer boughs with a white filigree in Sequoia National Forest, California, in the southern Sierra Nevada. Early-season hikers in these mountains experience the delights of winter scenery and perhaps such diversions as a camp-fire marshmallow roast; but they must also expect severe weather and broad expanses of snow cups (below), which result from uneven melting and make for treacherous footing.

17

Camped high on the rocky slopes of Mount Whitney in the Sierra Nevada, Will finds his drinking water frozen and shakes the bottle violently to break up the ice so he can make breakfast tea. Overtaken by darkness the previous night after 15 hours of up-and-down hiking—the most exhausting day of the trip—he and Sam Abell had bivouacked on the trail at 13,500 feet. The splendid, snowy heights of the Sierra (right), loftiest barriers of the entire Pacific Crest Trail, extend for more than half the length of California.

Backpacker relaxes in the kitchen doorway of a hotel in Lone Pine, California.

Many small-town inns welcome detouring hikers eager for a bath and a bed.

Crystal waters of the Sandy River plunge
over a tumbled wall of black volcanic
rock to form Oregon's Ramona Falls
in the Mount Hood National Forest.
The Pacific Crest Trail passes within
a few feet of the base of the falls.
Near Paradise Park on the western
slope of Mount Hood, a clump of rush
(below) takes its flaming color from the
last rays of the setting sun.

In a six-month period from April to October 1974, Denise Myers and Hal Simmons of Colorado Springs, Colorado, walked the entire Pacific Crest Trail—two of only a handful of hikers that have covered all 2,400 miles. With time out for bad weather and a delay when thieves stole their packs, they averaged 17 miles per hiking day and sometimes went more than 20. Two companions fell out along the way. At the end Hal called the hike "a total experience—physical, mental, spiritual."

*Jutting above the Cascade ridges of southern Washington and northern
Oregon, the volcanic pyramid of Mount Hood reaches toward drifting
gray clouds. Morning sunlight gilds the Columbia River, boundary
between the two states and the lowest point on the Pacific Crest Trail.
Camped on the snowy flank of Mount Hood, Del Young, instructor
and guide for a mountaineering school, gazes into the lowering mist
and wonders if the weather will permit a climb to the top.*

SOUTHERN CALIFORNIA: CHAPARRAL AND PINES

1

FRAGRANT WITH SAGE, a riffling breeze played among low hills blanketed by chaparral. Standing near the brow of one incline, Sam and I cast long charcoal shadows in the amber light of an April sunrise.

Behind us a barbed-wire fence — the international boundary between the United States and Mexico — sliced arrow-straight across the land. Nailed to one of the fence posts near a crumbling customshouse was a small shield marking the southern end of the Pacific Crest Trail: a rounded triangle with snowy mountains and a black pine tree superimposed on a blue background, the trail's official emblem and the main route marker we would follow to Canada.

As the sun pushed higher, we hoisted our packs, touched the soil beyond the barbed wire in a salute to Mexico, and started north. In the first 70 yards we crossed a furrowed field and turned onto a narrow dirt road, the initial link in hundreds of miles of temporary trail route in southern California. For a mile we walked this dusty road to the sun-drenched village of Campo; from there the trail followed a paved road north.

Within a couple of hours the heat of the blacktop, the stiff unbroken leather of my new hiking boots, and the city-soft condition of my feet combined to produce blisters the size of half dollars on my heels. I would hobble with pain the next three weeks while these wounds gradually healed into calluses as tough as rawhide.

Before we had traveled even a dozen miles, we gained some insight into the problem the Forest Service faces in acquiring right-of-way for the trail. As with most questions, there are two sides to the issue. In a grove of live oaks, we called on Lester Hook, a short, sturdy man with a full head of blond hair under his sweat-stained cowboy hat. The soft-spoken rancher has been raising beef cattle for almost all his 65 years. "My widowed grandmother homesteaded here back in 1883," he said, "and the place has been in our family ever since. This land means a lot to me. I was born here and I intend to die here."

Palms and steaming pools mark the oasis of Warner Springs in southern California's Colorado Desert. Well known to Indians of ancient times, the hot mineral waters now ease the aches of hikers and other resort guests.

He invited us into the small, frame ranch house where his 70-year-old housekeeper, Winnie Dennis, served coffee in the pine-paneled sitting room. Rocking as he talked, he told us about his dispute with the Forest Service. "I own 480 acres, divided in two parcels by some federal land," he said. "I've leased that strip from the Government for the last 40 years, and it's some of the best grazing land I've got. But now the Forest Service wants to go right across that ground with a permanent section of the trail you boys are hiking."

I asked why hikers and cattle couldn't co-exist.

"It isn't just the hikers," was the answer. "I know the trail is supposed to be closed to vehicles, but ranchers around here have already had problems with trail bikes and dune buggies and even backpackers spooking the cattle. When a cow runs it drops weight, and that weight is money to us."

Lester saddled horses to show us the land involved. We pulled up where Buckman Springs Road crosses a bridge over dry Cottonwood Creek. "The Forest Service wants the trail to come through here, following the creek bed, but it's my best grazing area. My proposal is to build the trail parallel to the road here for a mile, then cut across my land to the north. It's not nearly as good grazing there, and I'm willing to let them have an easement across it."

That evening Lester and a dozen other ranchers confronted Don Smith, supervisor of the Cleveland National Forest, and John Caragozian, lands officer, at a meeting at Mountain Empire High School in Campo. "We've considered all the alternatives," Caragozian said firmly, "and we feel we've chosen the best route for the trail. There's no proof that people hiking across the meadow are going to be detrimental to a cattle-raising operation."

But the ranchers were adamant in backing Hook. Finally, Smith broke the deadlock by agreeing to explore Lester's proposal. "We recognize and appreciate the interest of the local people," he said. "We certainly don't intend to run anyone out of business. We'll see if we can get your idea approved, and do what we can to make it work."

Back at his ranch, Lester peered out through the darkness at the rolling hills. He turned to me and said, "I'm getting old now. All I want is to work a little and have some peace and quiet. They say it will be at least three years before the trail will be built. I hope it's at least that long."

North of the Hook ranch the trail winds toward the Laguna Mountains, whose slump-shouldered, eroded ridgeline rises a mile high. Before starting the climb, we paused beside Kitchen Creek—the first moving water we had encountered on the trail—to cool off in a stand of scrub oaks. The toothed, holly-like leaves of these compact trees provide some of the best shade in chaparral country. On the nearby slopes I could pick out silhouettes of the yucca called Spanish bayonet. A single stalk, several feet tall, juts from a cluster of long rigid, sharply pointed leaves. The forbidding armament of these leaves contrasts with the creamy white softness of the blossoms crowning the stalk.

As we climbed, the life zones changed, and near the top of the Lagunas we came on proof of increasing rainfall: small meadows and our first pine trees. Like all the mountains of the Pacific Crest, the Lagunas trap moisture-laden clouds moving inland from the ocean. *Ah-ha Kew-ah-mac*, Land of the Rain Beyond, the Diegueño Indians called these highlands.

Here, too, we found our first permanent, improved route, the five-mile Laguna Rim Trail. Toward evening we edged along the eastern escarpment where the Lagunas drop off precipitously to the floor of the Colorado Desert more than 4,000 feet below, and watched twilight transform the scene from a sere expanse of sand and jagged ridges into a realm of mystery; spreading shadows softened the hard edges, and the dying sun coaxed shades of blue, purple, and burgundy from the earth. As the last light drained from the sky, an owl leaped from a rocky outcrop and drifted away on widespread wings.

In deepening dusk we ambled along the Rim Trail as it curved through broad thickets of manzanita, low dense shrubs with smooth reddish bark, oval leaves, and deep red berries; the Spanish name means "little apple." After walking a couple of miles with only starlight to guide us, we made camp under the low branches of a Jeffrey pine. I propped my pack against its trunk, cleared away fallen pine cones, and spread my goose-down sleeping bag beneath a sweeping limb decked with curving five-inch needles. After supper Sam and I sat up late, gazing at a black sky dotted with icy white stars and listening to a soft wind rustling through the pines.

From the Laguna Rim the temporary trail descends into the cool forests of Cuyamaca Rancho State Park and crosses low hills east of Julian, scene of a gold rush in 1870 and now an important apple-growing center. Below Julian we came to the narrow San Felipe Valley, which slices between two rocky ridges; flat and grassy at the bottom, it tapers up to sagebrush and prickly pear cactus on the ridge slopes. An evening breeze danced through the quiet valley as we walked along the shoulder of a paved road. Only an occasional hay truck or pickup camper disturbed the serenity, zooming past and buffeting my pack with a blast of air. As night fell I heard the call of a coyote on the ridge high above, a haunting wail that lingered as an echo.

In the San Felipe Valley, the Pacific Crest Trail merges with history.

Beginning at a barbed-wire fence along the Mexico-United States border, the Pacific Crest Trail wends northward and upward. Crossing range-land and desert, it rises through low, rugged foothills before climbing above 9,000 feet on the flanks of Mount San Jacinto. After descending to dusty San Gorgonio Pass, the trail meanders up into the pines of the San Bernardino and San Gabriel Mountains.

On October 6, 1858, the first westbound stagecoach of the Butterfield Overland Mail Line rumbled up this valley on its way from Tipton, Missouri, to San Francisco — a journey that covered 2,700 miles in just under 24 days. For 2½ years, both westbound and eastbound stages passed through twice weekly, their determined drivers heeding the admonition of founder John Butterfield: "Remember boys, nothing on God's earth must stop the United States mail!"

In addition to the mail contract, Butterfield made money by carrying newspapers, packages, and passengers. Often as many as nine people, their baggage, and 600 pounds of mail were crowded into a single coach pulled by relays of teams of four to six horses. The travelers ate hurried, mostly unappetizing meals at the 165 stations along the way, and slept or tried to sleep in the bouncing coach. Some passengers were exhilarated by the experience, but most found it tedious and uncomfortable; one overwrought soul went mad.

At the head of the San Felipe Valley, the Butterfield Trail cut over a pass and headed west; the Pacific Crest Trail veers north, and it soon brought us to Warner Springs, an oasis fed by natural hot springs. For centuries, Cupeño Indians lived nearby and used these waters for their restorative powers. In 1844 Jonathan Trumbull Warner, a Connecticut Yankee who came west as a trapper, received from the Mexican government a grant of 44,000 acres that included the hot springs. In 1911 William G. Henshaw acquired the ranch and developed the present desert resort, long popular with coastal Californians.

On a hot, dusty afternoon, Sam and I approached Warner's Resort half-wondering if we were seeing a mirage. Large trees shaded lanes dotted with adobe cottages. Purple irises, brilliant orange California poppies, and fragrant lavender lilacs lined walkways where children played tag and young couples strolled hand-in-hand. Dozens of birds, including western bluebirds with their plumage of light orange and royal blue, sang in the trees.

General manager Dan Myles escorted me to the hot springs, where palm trees ringed a series of bubbling pools, and explained that 230,000 gallons of water flow out each day at an average temperature of 138° F. "From here the water is piped to our two swimming pools," he said. "We keep one at about 80° and the other at 105°. Most of the hikers who come through here seem to enjoy eating a big meal, sleeping in a bed, and soaking in the hot water." We were certainly no different from the others, and I especially appreciated the hot pool, which massaged my sore muscles and helped heal my blistered feet.

Loafing beside the springs, I met an aged Indian with a snow-white handlebar mustache, bushy white eyebrows, and a few strands of white hair. He wore jeans and a blue-striped cowboy shirt with pearl buttons. His name was Julio Ortega, and he was more than 100 years old.

"I was born just down the road here," he said in a surprisingly deep, gravelly voice. "For most of my life I worked as a vaquero around here and down in Arizona. I worked on cattle drives, I busted broncos, I chased strays. I was a little fellow when I started in; I guess it was almost 1900 before I really began to know something about cattle." His faded eyes closed as he reminisced. "Things were better then than they are now. All I do now is talk to people and lie on my bed and sleep."

The Henshaw family had acknowledged Julio's years of service to the Warner ranch by providing a house, food, and spending money for the old vaquero for the rest of his life.

I sought out Michael Linton, one of Julio's 29 grandchildren. "Yes, my grandfather's quite a man," he said. "He speaks English, Spanish, and several Indian dialects. Years ago he was a Diegueño chief, and during his life he has owned three ranches. He also owned one of the first automobiles in this area. I've heard rumors that he even started an entire second family of Ortegas down in Arizona."

That night Sam and I again sat up marveling at the stars. Through the clear air, far from city lights, they shone with a brilliance I never see near my urban home. Earlier we had noticed a metallic gleam atop a nearby ridge — reflection from the dome of Palomar Observatory, which houses the world's largest reflecting telescope. Now it was easy to understand why that site was chosen. We traced the outlines of constellations, watched stars swing below the horizon as the earth rotated, followed the streaks of meteors, and let our imaginations wander through the galaxies.

Next morning we left Warner Springs and headed for Mount San Jacinto, which soars to 10,804 feet and would be the first snow-capped peak of our trip. The trail climbs above 9,000 feet as it skirts the summit.

By the time we set foot in the San Jacinto Mountains, we had traveled about 135 miles from the border, and I decided that I was finally mastering the fine art of backpacking. My muscles, like my equipment, were nearly broken in. I had trimmed excess weight from my body and superfluous articles from my pack. Since Sam had 20 pounds of photographic equipment, I was carrying much of the community weight — tent, stove, pots — and I had learned to arrange the 50 to 60 pounds so the pack rode comfortably.

Sam and I had settled on a lightweight and fairly tasty diet: for breakfast, tea and granola with honey and powdered milk; for lunch, bouillon, dried fruit, chocolate, and a mixture of nuts, seeds, and candies; for supper, one of our own casseroles of freeze-dried chunks of chicken or beef, freeze-dried green beans, powdered gravy, and such seasonings as pepper, thyme, or tarragon. An orange, an onion, some cheese or bread added variety.

While hiking I found I was most comfortable wearing just shorts and boots. In the night chill I pulled on trousers and various combinations of cotton, wool, and goose down, depending on the temperature. I carried moccasins for camp shoes, and wore a brimmed hat for warmth or as a sunshade.

The daily schedule was flexible; we let events or terrain dictate distance and pace. Over the entire period our longest day covered 23 miles, the shortest 0; we averaged about 10 miles a day. We would start hiking in the cool of the morning, then take a long break for lunch followed by a nap and perhaps a swim in the middle of the day. After the heat started to abate, we would hike into evening, and sometimes spend as long as an hour finding the best available spot to camp. Level ground, accessible water, and an inspiring view were major considerations. Although I carried a two-man nylon tent, we only used it in severe cold, rain, or snow, both of us preferring to sleep under the stars.

I was also becoming more familiar with the geology, wildlife, and plants around us. As we climbed into the San Jacintos, we entered the realm of the pines — Coulter, ponderosa, sugar, Jeffrey, lodgepole. Mixed with the pines were incense cedars hung with mistletoe; later we saw white fir. Lizards scampered among the granite rocks at lower elevations. Squirrels and chipmunks were prevalent as we moved higher.

The trail switchbacked steeply up the side of Tahquitz Peak, named for an evil spirit feared by Cahuilla Indians. At 8,823 feet Tahquitz, topped by a fire lookout tower, forms a shoulder of Mount San Jacinto and stands just within the San Jacinto Wilderness. The Wilderness Act, passed by Congress in 1964, preserves such tracts of land that retain their "primeval character and influence, without permanent improvements or human habitation . . . with the imprint of man's work substantially unnoticeable. . . ." Today, some 11 million acres in 65 different tracts are protected under the act.

On the steep north side of Tahquitz, a large snowfield several feet deep concealed the trail. With an amateur's caution, I gingerly stepped from a rock onto the sloping snow. Immediately my feet slipped, the shifting weight of my pack threw me off balance, and I tumbled a dozen feet downhill. Wiser, I picked myself up, chopped a narrow ledge in the snow with the outside edge of my right boot, put my weight on it, and made another cut with the inside edge of my left boot. Using this method — which we would perfect in miles of snow in the Sierra Nevada — Sam and I took turns cutting the trail across the thousand-yard barrier.

We trudged down into the forested saddle between Tahquitz and San Jacinto as the sun was setting and the lights of Idyllwild, in a valley 2,000 feet below, came winking on. During the night a west wind pushed a thick bank of clouds our way, obscuring the stars and spreading a gray veil over dawn. Climbing again, we soon reached Strawberry Cienega, a meadow cut by several splashing streams. Fingers of ice still clung to nearby rocks and plants. By noon a warming sun had broken through the clouds, and we began to descend San Jacinto.

Dividing the San Jacinto Mountains from the San Bernardino Mountains to the north is a deep cleavage known as San Gorgonio Pass. At an elevation of only about 1,300 feet, it lies nearly two vertical miles below the summits on either side. A main route of early settlers, the pass today funnels freeway traffic between Los Angeles and Palm Springs. As we crossed under the highway a desiccating wind whipped through the great gap, blowing grit into my face and hair. I looked northward and saw the snowy hulk of San Gorgonio Mountain, highest of the San Bernardinos, only 15 miles away.

The trail winds just east of San Gorgonio, but the hiker who chooses can take a side trail to its summit and travel through six distinct life zones between the pass and the peak — the equivalent of moving, in terms of environment, from Mexico to the frozen expanses of Alaska.

Each life zone contains a community of living things that have adapted to certain conditions. One zone merges into another at a progressively cooler

"The stagecoaches of the Butterfield Mail Line rumbled up this valley . . ."

temperature range, determined by elevation (advancing up a mountain) or by latitude (moving farther north). The life zone at San Gorgonio Pass is the Lower Sonoran, dominated by desert plants. As the trail wanders up the Whitewater River and Mission Creek into the heights of the San Bernardinos, it ascends through Upper Sonoran, Transition, Canadian, Hudsonian, and Alpine-Arctic zones; from cactus to chaparral to conifer forest to sparse, hardy grasses and wild flowers to bare rock and ice.

San Bernardino National Forest is the most heavily visited in the United States. Bill Haire, San Jacinto District recreation and lands officer, told us why: "We're within a two-hour drive of the homes of ten million people, including the population centers of Los Angeles and San Diego. That means about half the people in California, the most populous state in the country."

The impact of that population is evident throughout the forest. As we followed the trail route along dirt roads, we met hundreds of recreational vehicles—trail bikes, jeeps, campers, motor homes. Throngs of vacationers crowded the shores of man-made Big Bear Lake and Lake Arrowhead, both near the trail.

I found respite from the people and cars, the motorboats and condominiums, along the cool quiet banks of Holcomb Creek. This small stream cuts through the mountains and nourishes a corridor of bright green in the midst of an often drab and dusty pine forest. Cottonwoods provided a leafy canopy for my enclave of solitude, and the only sound was the creek murmuring to the rocks as it tumbled over them.

West of Holcomb Creek, the trail goes up Lone Pine Canyon, a long straight valley that marks a segment of the 700-mile-long San Andreas Fault. A massive shift along the San Andreas caused the cataclysmic San Francisco earthquake of 1906.

In the middle of the flat, half-mile-wide canyon, Sam and I overtook a geology class on a field trip from nearby Riverside City College. Professor Bob Southwick was telling his 25 students, "The whole width of this canyon is the San Andreas Fault; it's not just a single seam in the rock, but a belt or zone of past fracturing and movement. It's called a rift valley.

"Along the San Andreas Fault, movement averages about two inches a

year. But it's not constant. The forces build up over a period of time, and when the stress becomes too much for the rock formations to resist, there's a quick, sharp adjustment — an earthquake." Then he reassured us. "There hasn't been an earthquake in Lone Pine Canyon in recorded history. Most likely it's not an active part of the fault."

We accompanied the class to a promontory that gave us a good view of the rift valley. Haze hung heavily over the San Bernardinos and nearly obscured the peaks of San Gorgonio and San Jacinto. "Smog . . . " Bob Southwick leaned on the word. "I've been coming up here on field trips for 12 years, and I've watched it get worse and worse. Now the smog is evident even on days that seem bright and clear."

I heard similar comments throughout the San Bernardinos and their sisters to the west, the San Gabriel Mountains. Richard Cernik, a 20-year veteran of the staff of Angeles National Forest, said, "It used to be as clear as crystal up here. If anybody had told me in the old days that there would be a smog problem in the San Gabriels, I would never have believed it."

To learn more about smog and its effects, Sam and I detoured from the crest of the San Gabriels to the city of Riverside, 50 miles east of Los Angeles in the mountain-rimmed Los Angeles Basin, a broad coastal plain.

"The particular topography here is part of the problem," said Paul Miller, a slim, intense plant pathologist for the Forest Service who works at the University of California's Air Pollution Research Center. "Smog is blown inland from the Los Angeles area and trapped by the mountains and the atmosphere's inversion layer. The heated mountain slopes act as a chimney to suck the polluted air from under the inversion layer up to the conifer forests.

"About 70 to 90 percent of the pollution is from automobile exhaust. Ozone, one of the products formed when exhaust fumes are irradiated by the sunlight, is toxic to trees and other living things. The ozone destroys the important photosynthesizing cells in pine needles; one immediate effect is a mottling or yellowing that works back from the tips of the needles. The amount of foliage is reduced, needles are shorter, the lower branches die out. The weakened trees are susceptible to bark beetles, which usually administer the coup de grâce. This is just one indicator of the imbalance imposed on the forest ecosystem by smog. Ponderosa and Jeffrey pine mortality rates have reached 4 percent annually in severely damaged sections of the San Bernardinos and San Gabriels."

Back in the mountains late that afternoon I came to a stand of young ponderosa pines. The ozone effects that Miller had described were plainly visible — dead branches, discolored needles. As I looked down between the ridges stretching toward the Los Angeles Basin, I saw a yellow haze hugging the lower slopes, thick and threatening. We make the smog, I thought; we have not learned to control it; and we are only gradually learning how far-reaching are its effects. Can we reverse the process? I looked again at the ponderosas and wished from my heart I knew how.

WHITE-LEAF MANZANITA

Vigorous and independent, 70-year-old Winnie Dennis keeps house for cattle rancher Lester Hook at his family homestead near the Mexican border —and also looks after any stray kitten that settles in the stable.

From the chaparral-lined Rim Trail in the mile-high Laguna Mountains, the author

looks eastward at sunrise over the ridges and valleys of the Colorado Desert.

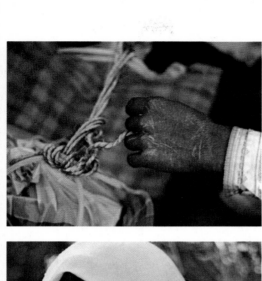

Tracked down by Border Patrol agents, illegal aliens assemble in single file. After crossing from Mexico at night, the men climbed Hauser Mountain and hid in the underbrush to get some rest. Caught while sleeping, they reacted with resignation. One waits matter-of-factly, arms folded; another ties up his bundle with chaparral-scratched hands. Sunlight filtering through a straw hat's brim speckles a solemn face. At far left, Agent Ron Busch shows Will one of the telltale footprints. The aliens come in search of work, and the Border Patrol captures about a thousand a month just in the vicinity of Campo, California.

*Dancers of the past smile
from a cantina wall at
Warner Springs. Julio
Ortega, a Diegueño Indian
more than 100 years old
when Sam took this photo-
graph, posed as the fiddler
for the mural when a resort
employee painted it in
1948. Julio began working
as a vaquero, or cowboy, on
a California ranch before
1900. During a long and
active career he owned
and operated three ranches.*

At a public meeting called by officials of Cleveland National Forest to discuss trail routing, lands officer John Caragozian recommends crossing land that Lester Hook has leased as part of his ranch for 40 years. Hook (opposite, left) and his housekeeper, Winnie Dennis, supported by other residents of the area, oppose the plan. Hook fears that some thoughtless trail users will seriously disturb his cattle. After examining alternatives, the Forest Service agreed to consider another route. Opposite, below, Hook passes Morena Reservoir while riding near the area under dispute.

Concerned rancher: Lester Hook favors hiking trails, but insists that rights

of nearby residents be protected.

"*This land means a lot to me. I was born here and I intend to die here.*"

MOJAVE SUN,
WHITNEY SNOW

2

"I THINK," said Christopher Robin, "that we ought to eat all our Provisions now, so that we shan't have so much to carry."

Every time I lifted my food-heavy pack at the start of a hike, I agreed with Winnie-the-Pooh's young friend. In the Mojave Desert that perpetual quandary — weight versus conservation of supplies — was magnified, for we had to carry all our water. At 8.33 pounds per gallon, the two gallons each that Sam and I carried overburdened our already ponderous packs.

The Mojave shimmered with heat as I scanned it from the Portal Hills, a low ridge northwest of the San Gabriel Mountains. The temporary trail route crosses 60 miles of this vast expanse of sand, rock, and scattered plants infrequently interspersed with irrigated fields. The permanent route is tentatively mapped through the dry, brown Tehachapi Mountains north of the Mojave. Officers of the Tejon Ranch Company, which owns more than 270,000 acres in this area, are negotiating with the Forest Service on a right-of-way across the ranch, one of the largest pieces of private property in California.

A strong wind from the west swept the floor of the Mojave and made walking in the 100° temperature just bearable. Here in the desert Sam and I met some of our first fellow hikers on the Pacific Crest Trail, the self-styled Drew Expedition: bearded Skip Drew; tall, thin Fred Burt, Jr.; and diminutive Jeff Lapham. During the next few months we would encounter them several times, and on each occasion one or more of the trio would be lost in meditation or absorbed in scrutinizing the surroundings. "To me," Skip explained, "it's not how far you walk, but what you see as you go. I'd rather spend my time staring into the waters of a stream than in hiking 20 miles a day."

In the middle of the Mojave, a line of squat hills rose above the horizon. One stood out distinctly because of its deep red color, a clue to its mineral content. Between 1894 and 1956, Tropico Hill yielded several million dollars worth of gold.

Precarious footbridge spans the torrent of Nine Mile Creek near Casa Vieja Meadow in the southern Sierra Nevada. Swollen by melting snow, mountain streams become time-consuming obstacles in spring and early summer.

Although the Tropico Mine produced its last gold nearly two decades ago, owners Glen and Dorene Settle have kept the place alive as a museum. They offer tours of the mine and recovery mill and have established Tropico Gold Camp, a replica boomtown community, at the foot of Tropico Hill. The authentic old buildings—from schoolhouse to saloon—come from historic mining towns throughout the West.

"Tropico was a typical hard-rock mining operation," Glen said as we entered the mine. The hot Mojave sun quickly gave way to the cool dark of the tunnel, part of a 12-mile network. "The gold was locked into quartz which, while it was still molten, worked into cracks in older rocks. To mine this ore you look for a vein of quartz and tunnel into it—like digging out the frosting between two layers of cake."

From the mine—a shaft that drops 900 feet with horizontal tunnels at nine levels—the quartz was transported in railborne ore cars to the nearby recovery mill, where crushers pounded the rock into dust and a chemical process removed the gold. In one room a blazing furnace melted the metal. "Then came the part I liked best," said Glen, "seeing molten gold and silver poured into 85-pound bars. But that represented a lot of work. Ten tons of quartz ore produced only enough gold to cover the palm of your hand."

Next morning we rejoined the temporary trail where it merges with the Los Angeles Aqueduct, which carries water 338 miles from the Sierra Nevada to Los Angeles. We camped near the aqueduct—covered to protect the water from pollution—in a forest of Joshua trees, the most distinctive plants I found along the entire trail. Each thick trunk supports branches contorted into strange shapes; at the end of each branch is a cluster of tough, foot-long green spines, rigid and needle sharp. As the tree grows, older spines die and fold back on the branches, forming a scaly armor over the wood. Some Joshuas live more than two hundred years. According to legend, they were named by Mormon settlers who saw in the upraised branches a suggestion of Joshua pointing to the Promised Land.

I fell asleep under the maze of branches and spines of an 18-foot Joshua tree. Early the next morning the temperature was already 70° as we walked toward the town of Mojave. From 1883 until 1888, teams of 20 mules lumbered into the railroad yard at Mojave to complete a ten-day, 165-mile haul across the desert from Death Valley. Each team pulled a train of three wagons. One contained a tank of water; the other two were immense vehicles with rear wheels seven feet high, and each held up to 23 tons of borax, valued then as now for its use in various chemical processes and products.

In the 20 miles between Mojave and Jawbone Canyon, the temporary trail crosses a wild, nearly uninhabited section of desert. The designated route follows the Southern Pacific railroad tracks, but Sam and I elected to walk cross-country, a decision that soon placed us in the midst of the desert ecosystem. Surrounding us in a vast province of blue sky and brown earth was a scattering of bur sage and creosote bushes accented by an infrequent Joshua tree. The wind blew almost constantly; when it did die down for a moment, sweat poured from my body, and flies buzzed around my face.

I quickly learned that, far from being empty and barren, the desert is home to myriad life forms. Under almost every creosote bush I spotted the burrow of an antelope ground squirrel. Half a dozen kinds of lizards flicked across the earth at startling speed. Horned toads looked deceptively fierce with their rough scales and horny crests. Passing by one creosote bush, I was startled by a dual explosion that produced a black-tailed jackrabbit and a bird that disappeared in a blur of wings.

Constantly I scanned the ground ahead for rattlesnakes. Like many people, I carry an exaggerated fear of snakes that my reason tries to whittle away. But reason gave way to near-panic the half dozen times I confronted snakes—including two menacing rattlers, each more than three feet long.

Before dusk we stopped in the lee of a six-foot creosote bush. As I was fixing supper, I noticed what looked like a slowly moving rock. Sam investigated and found it to be one of the most venerable of desert dwellers, a tortoise. The foot-long creature abruptly disappeared within its gray-brown shell, but eventually its wrinkled, saggy face poked out again. With beady eyes it studied us for a moment, then continued on its slow, patient journey.

Sam was photographing desert plants the next day when I heard someone call. I turned and was amazed to see a pretty young blond woman running toward us. "Hi! I'm Betty Shaneyfelt," she gasped as she came up, breathless from her dash. "My family lives over there"—she pointed to a distant cluster of trees—"and we want you to eat with us."

We gladly accepted, and soon we were drinking fresh goat's milk and eating homemade cheese at the hospitable table of Bob and Maggie Shaneyfelt, parents of nine attractive young people. "I've always taught my children to be

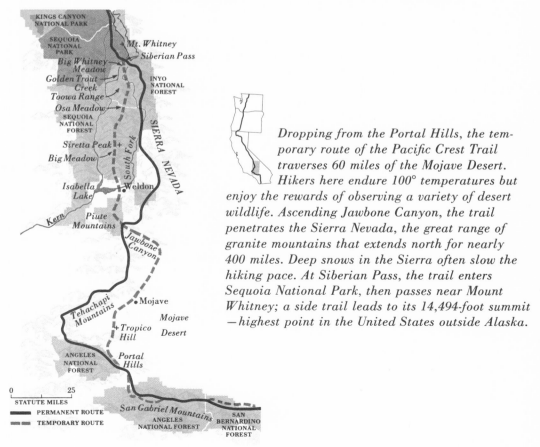

Dropping from the Portal Hills, the temporary route of the Pacific Crest Trail traverses 60 miles of the Mojave Desert. Hikers here endure 100° temperatures but enjoy the rewards of observing a variety of desert wildlife. Ascending Jawbone Canyon, the trail penetrates the Sierra Nevada, the great range of granite mountains that extends north for nearly 400 miles. Deep snows in the Sierra often slow the hiking pace. At Siberian Pass, the trail enters Sequoia National Park, then passes near Mount Whitney; a side trail leads to its 14,494-foot summit —highest point in the United States outside Alaska.

open to people, and that includes strangers," said Bob, who teaches art in Mojave. "One of the easiest ways to learn things in this life is from others. If you shut yourself off from them, you're the loser."

As we neared the northern limits of the Mojave, I searched the horizon for a glimpse of the snow-covered heights of the Sierra Nevada. Pushing ahead of Sam, who occasionally detoured in response to a photographic challenge, I entered Jawbone Canyon—a dusty, eroded area scored by the tracks of hundreds of trail bikes—passed through meadowed Kelso Valley, and then climbed long Geringer Grade into the Piute Mountains.

Almost before I realized it, my environment had changed entirely. Now some 4,000 feet higher than the Mojave, I found myself walking through pines and buffeted by a wind sharp with a wintry chill. A fallen tree blocked the wind but not the cold, and I crawled into my sleeping bag an hour before sunset. I awoke on a cloudy morning to discover ice in my plastic water bottle.

I dropped out of the Piutes into a more familiar climate along the South Fork of the Kern River: The temperature soared above 90° as I entered the village of Weldon (some fellow hikers dubbed it Well-done) not far from Isabella Lake. At his home nearby I visited Dr. Rene Engel, a distinguished 87-year-old geologist, to learn about the formation of the Sierra Nevada.

"You must understand," he said with a melodic French accent, "that a mountain range is created by a series of complex geologic events. More than 200 million years ago, this area was covered by a vast sea that deposited layer upon layer of marine sediments. Later these hardened and were folded and faulted. Then molten granite was intruded under the sediments in such volume that it formed massive bodies called plutons. Gradually, the mass was uplifted and many of the sedimentary layers were eroded away, exposing the granite.

"Within the last 15 million years the granite was lifted and tilted by faults to its current shape—precipitous to the east, gently sloping to the west. The Sierra range, you see, is a continuous block of granite nearly 400 miles long and some 50 to 80 miles wide. My advice to you," Dr. Engel concluded as I left his study, "is to be alert as you walk through the mountains. You will learn much more geology from them than you will from me."

But trudging through Big Meadow, an open expanse in the highlands northeast of Isabella Lake, Sam and I were more concerned with snow than with rocks. An overnight spring storm had dumped five inches of fresh powder, and a steely sky threatened more. The fine, dry snow drifted to depths of two feet and clung to my boots and pants. By the time we had crossed Big Meadow my feet were numb.

The trail climbed out of the meadow, following a fork of Salmon Creek through a forested glen, and we were surrounded by the serenity of a wilderness snowscape. Every needle of every conifer was outlined with a delicate filigree of snow; every rock had a cap of white. The only sound other than the crunching of our boots was the creek, mumbling along its icy course.

At an 8,820-foot-high pass below rocky Siretta Peak, we cleared a campsite near a stand of manzanita. We set up the tent as a defense against the cold; the temperature that day never climbed above freezing. With my ice ax I chopped through a thickening silver layer on the creek and drew some water. That night was one of the coldest of our trip; the temperature inside the tent dropped to 10°, and I shivered even inside my goose-down sleeping bag.

A cheering sun brightened the morning and soon began melting the fresh snow. Two days later, only the remnants of the old winter snowpack remained. Still, these were considerable. In the pine forests of the southern Sierra, snowbanks several feet high and dozens of feet across blocked the trail. At first I enjoyed clambering up one side and glissading down the other, but as water invaded my boots and chilled my feet, I began to avoid the snow. This caused a different problem: Often the trail would veer off in another direction under the snow, and I would have to search a wide sector to find it.

The meadows that interspersed the forest were saturated by spring run-off, and where the trail was free of snow it was often an inch or two deep in running water or a path of soggy moss or slippery mud. The swollen streams spilled over their banks and were often difficult to ford.

We could jump across Osa Creek, however, where it entered sloping Osa Meadow. On a hillock above the meadow we made camp, and soon we were joined by a solitary hiker. Tall and slender, with wavy brown hair and a thick mustache, he introduced himself as Kevin O'Leary, part-time writer, part-time San Francisco taxi driver. He had started hiking at the Mexican border and was bound for Yosemite. We sat up late around the fire, and I asked Kevin what impelled him to hike such a long section of the Pacific Crest Trail.

"Just the experience," he answered. "You know, hiking an unfamiliar trail is something like traveling through a foreign country. Every night you're in a new and strange place. But by the time you've eaten and found a place to sleep, you feel right at home, and you always hate to leave in the morning."

A choir of frogs sang hoarse lullabies far into the night, and a heavy frost coated Osa Meadow. Luckily I anticipated it, and slept under the sheltering branches of a pine. Kevin, however, slept out where the dew settled on him, and in the morning a thick white rime encrusted his sleeping bag.

Kevin decided to hike with us for a while, and we resumed the routine of dodging snowbanks and crossing sodden meadows. The vale called Casa Vieja was so wet that it sparkled like gold in the sun. In Long Canyon a creek had inundated a small meadow with a sheet of water three inches deep. Foot-long blades of grass, pushed horizontal by the water, undulated in the current like willow branches waving in a breeze.

Long Canyon led to the crest of the Toowa Range, a jagged ridge offering our first vista of the High Sierra: that chain of bare, windswept cliffs and crags that jut above timberline, peak on snowclad peak, a desert of white snow and gray granite rising higher than 14,000 feet. *"Una gran sierra nevada,"* a great snow-covered range, Spanish missionary Pedro Font recorded in 1776 when he first sighted these mountains.

At Golden Trout Creek, I stretched out on a log that had fallen across the water and watched seven-inch golden trout play among the shadows. The species originated in streams in this region, acquiring over the centuries the yellow and red hues of the volcanic earth. Popular with fishermen, golden trout have now been planted in high lakes and streams throughout the Sierra. As I watched the water and the fish, a teen-age angler came along and proudly showed me his catch of five goldens. He could hardly wait to eat them, insisting they were the tastiest of trout.

A short distance upstream Golden Trout Creek formed a roaring cataract over tumbled boulders. Just beyond we rounded a bend and entered Big Whitney Meadow, walled at the north by the gray-brown Sierra massif. Sunlight and clouds played over the high peaks. In the sun the mountains seemed friendly and inviting; in shadow they turned forbidding and vaguely threatening.

We camped at the south end of the meadow among stunted pines. It was getting cold, and I went to bed early. Sometime in the night I awoke with my heart pounding; a series of chilling howls and barks announced that a pack of coyotes had encircled our camp. Equally startled, Kevin and Sam tensely listened with me as the clamor continued for several minutes, then abruptly ended. I had read that coyotes never attack humans, but somehow that knowledge was less than reassuring, and I lay awake the rest of the night.

We kept the same campsite that day, waiting for Doug Gosling and a new supply of food. Doug is a college student from Toledo, Ohio, to whom Sam once taught photography in high school. He was now on his summer vacation and had agreed to assist us with such matters; he was backpacking in over a side trail to meet us here. Doug, whose Scandinavian heritage shows in his platinum hair and blue eyes, is a botany major, and he would teach me much about plants in the coming weeks. He arrived that afternoon, and we celebrated with a dozen fresh, sticky cinnamon buns that topped his pack.

Next morning Doug left to retrace his steps to our supply van, then to leapfrog north to another rendezvous point, while Sam, Kevin, and I climbed toward Siberian Pass, southern portal of the High Sierra. It was a bright, chill day, and I walked to the cadence of woodpeckers through a forest spangled with snowbanks and sparkling water. I thought of something Mark Twain wrote of these mountains: "The air up there . . . is very pure and fine, bracing and delicious. And why shouldn't it be?—it is the same the angels breathe."

After an hour's climb we entered the zone of the distinctive foxtail pine. Its thick corrugated bark is a deep reddish brown. Short needles, in clusters of five, grow only on the last 10 to 20 inches of the small branches in a formation that resembles the tail of a fox, especially when stirred by a breeze. Ancient foxtails have been found that have been living 1,500 years—probably the oldest trees along the trail.

We crested at nearly 11,000 feet and looked out over aptly-named Siberian Outpost, a harsh, bare plain blanketed with white. Above the Outpost reared several monolithic peaks, and I knew that just beyond rose Mount Whitney, crown of the Sierra.

At the southern boundary of Sequoia National Park, Siberian Pass marks the start of 250 miles of permanent Pacific Crest Trail. Much of this section was still under snow in May and June, and we soon became accustomed to following the route by reference to topographic maps and guidebooks. Donning

"No hiker commanded a loftier vantage, a more stunning panorama."

gaiters — short leggings that help keep snow out of boot tops — Kevin, Sam, and I slogged across the Outpost and waded through hip-deep drifts down to Rock Creek. We crossed it safely on a slippery log, and then climbed to an 11,000-foot pass on the shoulder of Mount Guyot. The sun had set when we found a clearing just large enough for our sleeping bags. Kevin built a fire and we dried our socks and boots, soaked after a full day of walking through snow.

At first light, while the surface was still firm, we crunched across Guyot Flat. In the lead, I estimated where the trail must angle along a snowy slope, and cut across it. After half an hour I stopped for a rest, and realized that Kevin and Sam were not in view behind me. We often lost sight of one another temporarily while hiking, but now I waited and no one appeared. Guessing that they might have headed toward Crabtree Meadow, where the side trail to Mount Whitney veers east from the Pacific Crest, I took a cross-country course for the meadow; there I searched in vain for fresh footprints in the mud. At the trail junction I waited and worried for two hours, imagining everything from equipment problems to a serious accident.

I decided to walk the mile to Crabtree Ranger Station but it, too, was deserted. Then, as I was debating where to look next, Sam and Kevin appeared, haggard but uninjured. "After we got separated from you," Sam explained, sprawling on the ground, "we started down a creek. We walked at least two miles before we decided we were off course and headed back up."

Reunion cheered us all, and in midafternoon we resumed our climb toward Mount Whitney, this time staying close together. Our route followed Whitney Creek through a U-shaped canyon carved out countless centuries ago by a glacier and flanked by towering rock fortresses. The snow grew deeper as we passed two frozen lakes, shining aquamarine in the clear mountain light. Near the second lake the valley widened, and I was humbled by the massive prominence ahead: a steep, jagged expanse of gray-brown rock, riven by snow-filled avalanche chutes, rising to rugged pinnacles 2,500 feet above me. I felt fragile and vulnerable before the enduring might of Mount Whitney.

The lower flanks lay deep in snow, cut here and there by the remains of rockslides. To reach the lowest switchback in view required us to angle steeply

up a snowfield. The deep snow was soft in the afternoon sun, and I kept breaking through the surface, often sinking to my hips. Struggling mired me even more. Twenty-five pounds heavier than either Sam or Kevin, I broke through with much greater frequency, and the exertion of repeatedly pulling myself out in the thin air at 13,000 feet soon exhausted me.

When we reached the first of the rockslide columns, I decided I would rather climb rock than snow, and began scrambling up the unstable stairway. Sam and Kevin chose to continue on the snow. The rockslide route grew steeper and narrower, and finally disappeared. I gingerly crossed a steep section of snow to the next parallel rock slope, using my ice ax for balance; struggling up the talus, I soon reached the elevation of the switchback. But an almost vertical snowfield still separated me from my goal. Stepping out onto the white surface, I immediately broke through. Loose snow tumbled down the slope, gathering speed as it plunged toward the valley hundreds of feet below. I slowly extracted myself, convinced that most of my strength had deserted me. After a few more steps I stumbled, lost my balance, and started to slide. I flailed out with the ice ax, chopping it downward into the snow; it held firm and jerked me to a halt. As my senses cleared I realized that a purely reflex action had saved me from a dangerous and possibly fatal fall.

A surge of adrenaline pushed me the remaining distance to the trail, where Sam was waiting. By now the sun was setting and my strength was ebbing with it. I convinced Sam, who still felt strong, that we should bivouac for the night. I drank hot bouillon, put on every piece of clothing I had, unrolled my sleeping bag right on the rocky pathway, and promptly fell asleep.

The night's rest renewed my strength, but a 20° temperature froze our water and our boots, and we were delayed for two hours while they thawed inside our sleeping bags. When we caught up with Kevin, who had camped some distance ahead of us, we found him plagued by some of the weakness and dizziness of altitude sickness. He and Sam decided to eat breakfast before starting to climb, while I went ahead to test the Whitney approach.

Hard snow alternated with exposed trail to make climbing easier than before, but I still had to pull for every breath. The higher I went, however, the more eager I became, and when a distant stone hut near the summit came into view, I pushed on.

A final switchback brought me to the rockbound top of Mount Whitney. The only snow on its windswept crown was inside the shelter, packed to the ceiling; apparently the door had been left open all winter. I scrambled over the huge slabs that form the mountain's ultimate pinnacle, and found a bench mark recording the elevation at 14,494.164 feet — highest point in the United States outside Alaska. At that moment, I realized, no other Pacific Crest Trail hiker commanded a loftier vantage, a more stunning panorama. Balanced on the topmost rock, I felt exultant.

FOXTAIL PINE

*Hungry rattlesnake disappears through the doorway of an
antelope ground squirrel's burrow in the Mojave Desert. In some 60
miles of desert walking, Sam and Will saw only half a dozen
poisonous snakes; both hikers and snakes kept a discreet distance.*

Sheltered by a venerable multi-branched Joshua tree, a camper stirs as morning comes to the Mojave. Soon the temperature will soar to 100° or more, but a brisk breeze often tempers the discomfort, and hikers find the activity and variety of desert wildlife fascinating. "We saw more living creatures here than anywhere else on the trail," Sam reported, listing horned toads and other lizards, ground squirrels, rabbits, coyotes, birds, and tortoises—one of which took refuge under a creosote bush (below) at the end of the day.

Tropico Gold Camp, a museum ghost town of vintage buildings, offers a muted echo of livelier days when the Tropico Mine yielded millions of dollars in gold. After production became uneconomic in 1956, mine owner Dorene Settle (opposite) and her husband developed the museum by moving authentic stores, saloon, schoolhouse, and furnishings from other mining towns. Here she pauses on the stairs of the mill to explain the recovery process. A protective asbestos mask hangs from machinery that once formed molten gold into ingots.

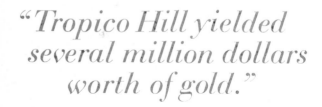

"*Tropico Hill yielded
several million dollars
worth of gold.*"

Gold still gleams at Tropico during the annual panning contest in March. Supplied with pans of gravel salted with a specified number of nuggets, competitors vie to find and separate them in the shortest time. Gold secure in his right hand, Joe L. Pauley (above) washes out his pan to finish second in the 1974 finals. Susie Kopp (opposite), 14, carries off the junior division trophy. The judges, old gold-panners all, compare results before awarding the "world championship" trophy (opposite, top); its miniature prospector holds a pan brimming with $500 worth of nuggets.

Last heavy snowfall of the year brings a
winter stillness in May to the woodlands of
the Kern Plateau in Sequoia National
Forest. A snowplant (above) pushes through
the ground to herald the arrival of spring;
soon it will erupt in a flamboyant display of
fire-red blossoms. Oddly, some field guides
list it as an ancient Indian remedy for
toothache while others brand it as poisonous.
Fallen pine cones (below) emerge as the
spring thaw warms the forest.

Bowed by exhaustion, Will rests heavily on his ice ax while crossing a snowy slope of Mount Whitney. The day began for him and Sam atop a distant ridge; from midafternoon until sundown, they slogged through hip-deep snow (below) in an attempt to reach the Whitney summit by nightfall. "The sun and soft snow, the altitude and thin air were all against us," said Will. "Finally we camped right on the trail."

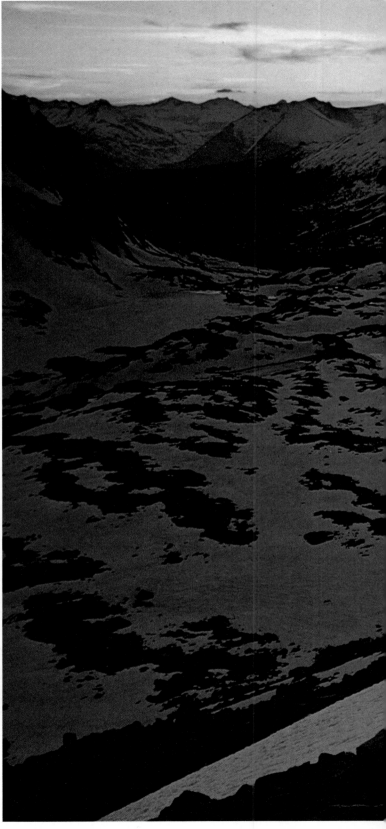

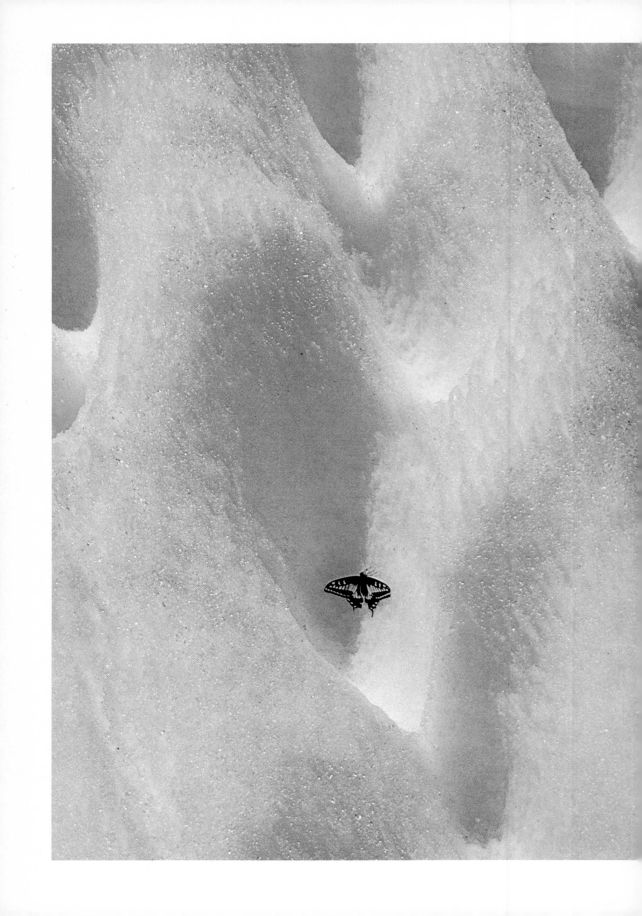

HEART OF THE SIERRA, THE "RANGE OF LIGHT"

3

"GOING TO THE MOUNTAINS is going home," John Muir once wrote. A quiet naturalist who became a fiery crusader for wilderness preservation, Muir lived in enduring kinship with his beloved forests and peaks, meadows and lakes of the Sierra Nevada.

Born in Scotland, this man with the craggy face, flowing beard, and penetrating blue eyes came to California in 1868 and stayed for most of the next half century — until his death in 1914. Carrying little more than his notebook, some dried bread, and a few tea leaves, he would ramble for a week or more at a time through the mountains. There he defined his creed — "Wildness is a necessity" — and he spent the rest of his life spreading the gospel that "mountain parks and reservations are useful not only as fountains of timber and irrigating rivers, but as fountains of life." Muir's poetic words captivated the nation and his energy spearheaded the establishment of several splendid national parks, including Sequoia, Kings Canyon, and Yosemite.

Although his travels took him far from California, he always returned to the Sierra which, he insisted, "should be called not the Nevada, or Snowy Range, but the Range of Light. And after ten years spent in the heart of it, rejoicing and wondering, bathing in its glorious floods of light, seeing the sunbursts of morning among the icy peaks, the noonday radiance on the trees and rocks and snow, the flush of the alpenglow, and a thousand dashing waterfalls with their marvelous abundance of irised spray, it still seems to me above all others the Range of Light, the most divinely beautiful of all the mountain-chains I have ever seen."

Muir's legacy endures: in the Sierra Club, the conservationist organization he founded in 1892; in the countless wilderness enthusiasts, including thousands of young people, who each year meditate on his writings; and in the John Muir Trail, a 212-mile pathway winding from the top of Mount Whitney to Yosemite Valley through the heart of the Sierra.

In colorful contrast to the snow, a swallowtail butterfly rests at the bottom of a snow cup formed by partial thawing. Sam spotted the unexpected visitor 11,500 feet high in the Sierra Nevada, just below Pinchot Pass.

For the second time within a few days, I found myself climbing toward the pinnacle of the Range of Light, this time in the company of Merrill Windsor, managing editor of this book. A sturdy, deliberate hiker, Merrill had joined me for a week on the trail while Sam flew home to Washington to review the film he had shot and Kevin continued north from Mount Whitney.

At sundown, as we bivouacked in a level area high above timberline, steel-gray clouds dumped a curious form of precipitation neither of us had ever seen before. A hybrid of sleet, snow, and hail — half-inch-thick puffs that looked and felt like soft foam plastic — peppered us for half an hour.

Long before sunrise we were trudging up the final mile to Whitney's summit, pausing frequently to labor for breath in the high, thin air. At the top, a cold wind plucked at our clothing as we congratulated each other. With the peak all to ourselves, we gazed out over the Sierra and eastward across the Owens Valley to the Inyo Mountains.

My pride in twice climbing Mount Whitney moderated a bit when I thought about Norman Clyde, who scaled the peak some 50 times. A legendary figure of the Sierra, Clyde is credited with 200 first ascents and more than a thousand climbs of California peaks higher than 10,000 feet, including the first "fresh-air traverse" of Whitney. The route "has that name," Clyde explained, "because there's a place where you take a rather long step with nothing but a thousand feet of fresh air below."

Almost until his death in 1972 at the age of 87, Norman Clyde seemed indefatigable. On his long hikes he carried a pack weighing a hundred pounds and containing, among other things, three pairs of special-purpose boots; five cameras; a library of small hardbound books in various languages; several guns; and an astonishing assortment of pots, pans, skillets, and kettles. "After a toilsome climb on the 10th of July," he once recorded, "up the rough abandoned trail over Harrison Pass at an elevation of 12,000 feet above the sea, I set down my heavy pack and looked about for a mountain to climb."

Finally Merrill and I left our matchless vantage and began the long, switchbacking descent to the glacial valley below. To my surprise the snow, so overpowering a week before, had melted considerably, and several previously frozen lakes were now ice-free and sparkling in the sun.

Another puffed-ice storm hit us where the John Muir Trail rejoins the Pacific Crest, and we camped in the protection of a group of tall pines. On a brisk, clear morning we crossed Sandy Meadow and soon reached a moraine, a low hill of earth, gravel, and rocks formed by a glacier that scraped material from the ground and shoved it aside as it slowly moved down the slope.

We passed several other moraines on the way to Wallace Creek, swollen with snowmelt and running 40 feet wide. Not relishing the thought of fording, I slowly removed my boots and socks, tied the laces together, slung the boots around my neck, and stepped into the swirling water. The shock of the sudden cold stole my breath and I nearly slipped on the slick cobbles underfoot. The water hit me at mid-thigh and splashed even higher, and the strong current forced me to angle downstream. Finally, I reached the north bank. As I rubbed life back into my numb legs, I watched Merrill begin his cautious crossing.

Halfway across, he stepped on an unstable rock; it tipped and he staggered, swayed for a moment, then fell forward; in an instant everything but his head and part of his pack was submerged. Fighting the current, he scrambled to his feet, gave me a wave and, heedless of another fall, lurched across the rest of the channel—emerging the wettest editor I have ever seen.

While he dried out, we talked to two hikers who were breaking camp beside the stream. Jim and Steve McWilliams, brothers from Fresno, California, were on a two-week backpacking vacation. "We've taken many short trips in the mountains, but this time we're hoping to cover at least a hundred miles," said Jim, a slim, bearded man of 27 who wore a red bandana around his head. "We came early in the season to avoid the crowds," added Steve. A college student, he was sketching a tree as we talked.

Beyond Wallace Creek a series of ridges brought the four of us to Bighorn Plateau, a broad expanse of earth and snow broken by a half-thawed lake. At the north end of the plateau we walked past a stand of foxtail pines, contorted into arthritic shapes by the force of the west wind.

We forded gushing Tyndall Creek without mishap, and began a 2,000-foot climb to the loftiest point on the Pacific Crest Trail: 13,200-foot Forester Pass. All afternoon we labored uphill with the pass enticingly in view, a tiny notch like a gunsight in a massive wall of gray granite. Near dusk we reached a bald knoll, still far below the pass, and stopped for the night. On a rock ledge I fell asleep surrounded by an austere landscape of rock, snow, and sky.

At daylight we began our final assault on Forester Pass, anxious to reach the top before the snow softened. But we found that the soles of Merrill's boots were too smooth to provide traction on the steep, crusted snowfield. Jim offered a set of crampons—foot spikes for climbing on ice—and after strapping these to his boots, Merrill had no more difficulty scaling the slope.

Near the top we reached trail sections that had been blasted out of the rock wall. Several switchbacks brought us to a point just a few dozen feet below the notch of Forester Pass, but to reach it we had to cross a nearly vertical snow-filled avalanche chute that dropped several hundred feet. Steve

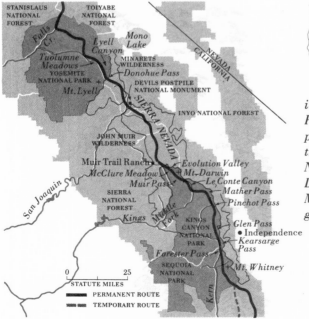

Scaling rockbound passes and fording swift streams, the Pacific Crest Trail crosses three national parks in the High Sierra. At Forester Pass, the trail reaches its highest point: 13,200 feet. Passing through the wonderland of Devils Postpile National Monument, hikers climb Donohue Pass, continue past glaciered Mount Lyell, and drop into the grassy vale of Tuolumne Meadows.

71

volunteered to cut steps up the chute; balancing precariously on his ice ax, he chopped into the snow with his boots a step at a time until he reached the pass. Following him, I fully appreciated his efforts, for I had trouble simply climbing in his footsteps.

A warming sun greeted us at the narrow pass, and we took a long break. Here at the trail's highest point, my mind wandered far north and I realized that I would descend more than 13,000 feet to reach the Columbia River between Oregon and Washington—at 173 feet the lowest elevation on the trail.

At 8:30 in the morning the snowfields extending north from Forester Pass were already so soft that Jim once plunged in to chin level. The sun blazed with an intensity that left us with various shades of sunburn. At the altitude we were hiking, the body receives nearly twice as much ultraviolet radiation as at sea level, and reflection from the snow adds its glare to direct sunlight.

Below the pass, we had to cross roiling Bubbs Creek on a snow bridge. This narrow span—four feet wide and two feet thick—looked too fragile to support both me and my pack and, as I began to shuffle across, I instinctively held my breath. A vivid vision of breaking through into the frigid maelstrom of the creek focused in my mind, but the bridge proved stronger than it looked. As we descended beside Bubbs Creek, the snow cover gradually lessened, but the flow of water grew to a frothy torrent. "In Arizona, where I come from," Merrill remarked, "that would be called a river." At Vidette Meadow, the creek widened and quieted, and we camped on a dry rise surrounded by green grass, tall trees, and tiny flowers — sharp contrast to our site of the night before.

Merrill and I left Jim and Steve McWilliams early the next morning and climbed the thousand-foot north wall of the Bubbs Creek canyon. Here we turned off the Pacific Crest Trail for Kearsarge Pass and a roadhead near the town of Independence, where Merrill departed for the East Coast. In his week of hiking he had satisfied himself "that I can still do something really physically challenging," and he had experienced some of the most spectacular country along the entire trail.

Sam was waiting at Independence, and two days later he and I hiked back up to windblown Kearsarge, one of a half dozen Sierra passes that were links on Indian trading routes. Tribes from east of the crest bartered such commodities as salt, piñon nuts, and obsidian for the shells, glass beads, and berries offered by the western tribes.

Surmounting wintry Glen Pass, we made camp between the two largest of the Rae Lakes. Sheets of ice 2 to 20 feet wide dappled the upper lake. I sat on a rock and watched the mini-ice-floes collide, slowly break up, and wash down the short channel connecting the lakes. The water surface between the drifting sheets of ice reflected the setting sun, and for a few minutes the lake became a tapestry of white and gold.

Under clear skies the wind blew crisp and cold as we continued northward past snowy peaks, ice-choked lakes, weather-twisted pines, and clusters of mountain heather — delicate rose blossoms atop six-inch evergreen stalks — and I marveled anew at the splendor of the wilderness.

Climbing to 12,110-foot Pinchot Pass—named for Gifford Pinchot, first chief of the U. S. Forest Service—we labored across broad snowfields dimpled with snow cups. These depressions, from several inches to three feet in depth, are formed by uneven thawing, and make a tedious and fatiguing barrier for hikers. After crossing a mile of such irregular hollows on a slope that grew steeper as it neared the pass, I was all but exhausted. The only momentary relief came when Sam spotted a handsome yellow and black swallowtail butterfly in the bottom of one depression. I wondered at our improbable luck in glimpsing that single touch of color among the thousands of empty snow cups we had passed.

A final hundred-foot-wide snowfield brought us to the top of Pinchot Pass, where we enjoyed another sweeping vista. "The only good thing about these passes," Sam said, "is that you can see yesterday's hike, then turn around and see tomorrow's."

We descended into the valley of the South Fork of the Kings River—a shortened form of the name bestowed in 1805 by Spanish explorer Gabriel Moraga: Rio de los Santos Reyes, or River of the Holy Kings—and followed it to its snow-filled headwaters below Mather Pass.

After an arduous climb, Sam and I glissaded down a steep slope, dropping nearly 800 feet in elevation in less than three minutes. At the bottom we plodded through snow to Palisade Lakes, nestled in a valley below the pinnacles of the 14,000-foot Palisades range. There we set up camp in the company of three chubby marmots. The inquisitive creatures waddled about searching for crumbs and trying to steal food from our packs.

Below Palisade Lakes the switchback trail descends a thousand-foot rock cliff on the so-called Golden Staircase. At the bottom, paralleling snow-lined Palisade Creek through a pine forest, we startled a grouse and her brood of six chicks. At the mother's alarmed clucks the youngsters scattered, running jerkily here and there like tiny windup toys. For the next 15 minutes she worked to regroup her family. Keeping a wary watch on Sam and me, she clucked constantly until she heard an answering peep, then escorted each chick to a hiding place.

Palisade Creek widened to a broad band of sparkling emerald, and Sam and I stopped for lunch in a grassy meadow shaded by quaking aspens. After a brief swim in the chill waters, I stretched out beneath a white-barked aspen and watched the distinctive leaves quiver in the slightest breeze. The gentle motion and the play of light on opposite sides of the leaves—bright green and gray-green—had a hypnotic effect, and I fell fast asleep.

Our route turned up the Middle Fork of the Kings River and took us into LeConte Canyon, a wooded cleavage among precipitous granite peaks. Partway through the canyon, a tangle of fallen trees embedded in snow blocked the trail. Apparently a late spring avalanche had thundered down from the heights, felling almost every tree in its quarter-mile-wide path. The needles, still green, gave off a fresh pine fragrance reminiscent of Christmas boughs as we clambered through the labyrinth of snarled branches and trunks.

At a small ranger station a hundred yards off the trail, we met two of the backcountry rangers who spend four months of the year in the wilderness of Sequoia and Kings Canyon National Parks. Gary Reichert, a broad-shouldered man with a sweeping mustache, is based at the LeConte Canyon Ranger Station; blond, blue-eyed Marv Evans has a cabin in McClure Meadow, 20 miles north.

Drinking tea sweetened with honey, we talked late into the night. "We're flown in by helicopter, with all of our supplies, around the first of June," Gary said. "Barring an emergency, we stay until the first of October. During that time the cabin is home, and that trail is the street in front of the house."

They talked about the people who travel past their ranger stations. "They're of all kinds," said Marv. "There are loners, and families, and scout troops. Happy people and sad people. People on strange trips — vows of silence, or off to set a new hiking speed record. There are a lot of people who underestimate the mountains. They live in a pretty secure world, and they assume that security extends to the wilderness."

"People don't understand that the mountains are indifferent," Gary mused. "There's nothing evil about mountains, they just don't care."

He walked with a limp as he moved about the cabin. "I think a spider must have bitten me," he said. "My foot puffed up, and it's so sore I can hardly walk on it." Weeks later, I learned that his condition continued to worsen and he had to be evacuated by helicopter for medical treatment. But at the time Gary's discomfort didn't seem serious, and Marv invited us to hike over Muir Pass with him when he returned to his station.

In the half-light of dawn, we set out through Little Pete and Big Pete Meadows, where we saw a dozen deer grazing on the dew-soaked grass. Rocky

*"Wildness
is a necessity."*

—JOHN MUIR

trail followed by steep snow brought us to Helen Lake, named — like Wanda Lake on the other side of the pass — for a daughter of John Muir. After angling up more long snow faces softening in the midday sun, I spotted the domed roof of Muir Hut, a small rock shelter built in 1931 at the top of Muir Pass.

We ate lunch at the hut, then edged along Wanda Lake and entered Evolution Basin — a broad, snow-filled glacial valley with three frozen lakes. A wall of mountains bounded its west side, rising into a sky of deep, pure blue.

In 1895 Theodore S. Solomons, a charter member of John Muir's Sierra Club, climbed into this barren basin. After studying the bordering peaks, he recorded in his journal, "I felt that here was a fraternity of Titans that in their naming should bear in common an august significance. And I could think of none more fitting to confer upon it than the great evolutionists, so at one in their devotion to the sublime in nature." Four of the peaks thus honor British scientists Charles Darwin, Thomas Huxley, Herbert Spencer, and Alfred Wallace — the major proponents of the theory of evolution.

Somber Evolution Basin drops steeply to the green swale of Evolution Valley, dotted with meadows. In the trees at the fringe of McClure Meadow, we found Marv's log cabin. Nine of the 20 miles we had hiked had been through snow, and I was bone weary. But our spirits rose when Doug appeared, walking in from the north to meet us. From his pack he pulled a whole series of treats: cheese, salami, thick-cut wheat bread, a bottle of wine, and, unbelievably, an entire German chocolate cake. After our banquet I went to bed and slept for 11 solid hours.

At noon, as Sam, Doug, and I were packing to leave, Marv announced, "I'm getting married soon, and I'd like to have you three come." He was planning a wilderness wedding at the Muir Trail Ranch, a resort only a mile off the Pacific Crest Trail and 13 miles northwest of McClure Meadow. Delighted at the invitation, we promised to attend.

We arrived at the guest ranch the day of the wedding in time for a hearty breakfast of cantaloupe, eggs, bacon, French toast, and strong coffee. In the log-walled dining room we met the bride, Jenifer Burckett, a slim woman with long brown hair and blue eyes.

As we ate, I talked with Karl Smith, owner of the ranch for 23 years. "I'm a mountain man at heart, I guess," Karl said, "although I've done a lot of different things in my life. I was a concert musician for 12 years with the Dallas Symphony, and I've worked as an inventor, designing surgical aids and auto safety devices. Having mechanical ingenuity sure helps around here."

At four that afternoon, wedding guests gathered on a granite outcrop near the South Fork of the San Joaquin River. As Karl played a wedding march on his baritone horn, Marv climbed to a ledge and watched Jenifer approach through a pine-shaded meadow on the arm of her father. She wore a handmade gown of light blue; her hair was interwoven with sprays of mountain Queen Anne's lace, and she carried a small bouquet of wild flowers.

Facing friends and relatives, bride and groom expressed their commitment to each other. "We believe," Jenifer began, "we have each found a person in whom we will always find joy and compatibility. By living and loving and working together, we intend to enrich our own lives as well as the lives of those who are our friends."

Marv continued, "Happiness and love in life are what we wish for each other, as well as for those around us." As Judge Darrel Day confirmed the marriage, Marv placed a ring on Jenifer's finger and held her close. For a moment the only sound was a slight rustling of the wind in the pine boughs overhead. Then, with the other guests, I followed the newlyweds to a grassy field. There they led us in a joyous and strenuous set of folk dances as we all earned our share of the wedding feast.

Days later and 50 miles north of Muir Trail Ranch, we entered Devils Postpile National Monument. Great pillars of basalt form an irregular cliff 60 feet high, reminiscent of a massive pipe organ; each column has several flat, smooth sides, and the individual shafts fit closely together. This amazing formation was created about a million years ago when a deep lava pool began to cool rapidly and solidify; the resulting shrinkage caused cracks that extended deep into the lava and produced the multi-sided pillars. Later a glacier moved across the area, shearing off part of the formation. I climbed to the top of the pillars, sliced level and then polished by the ice, and walked across a floor that resembles an intricate mosaic.

As Sam and I crossed a bridge over the Middle Fork of the San Joaquin and began to labor up a long dusty slope, it was clear that summer had finally overtaken us. The day was hot and sultry, the hikers were numerous, the mosquitoes were out in force.

Rounding a turn above Johnston Meadow, I caught my first glimpse of the Minarets, a serrated chain of sharp rock pinnacles some of which even John Muir found "inaccessible." Unstoppable Norman Clyde, however, made the first ascent of the highest Minaret, and it now bears his name.

A series of ridges dappled by lakes brought us to 11,056-foot Donohue Pass, at the boundary of Yosemite National Park. Compared to the higher passes farther south, Donohue seemed easy, and we reached the top almost before realizing it. Above us loomed Mount Lyell, its forbidding north wall smothered by Lyell Glacier, one of about 60 small glaciers in the Sierra. Far below, down a steep gorge, lay long-meadowed Lyell Canyon and the Lyell Fork of the Tuolumne River.

At dawn we made our way down to the gently sloping canyon. Dewy grass glistened in the sun, and I could smell the thick, rich earth. As we descended, the growth of summer was luxuriant around us, and we walked into Yosemite on a carpet of green.

Patiently scraping peanut butter from a nearly empty jar at her Yosemite campsite below Donohue Pass, Denise Myers observes a rule quickly learned by backpackers: Carry only what you need—and waste nothing.

ABOVE: ASPEN LEAF

Snowmelt thundering down Woods Creek tosses spray high above its rocky channel

in Kings Canyon National Park. The early-morning sun brightens Mount Clarence King.

With mountain wild
flowers as a bridal bou-
quet, Jenifer Burckett ac-
cepts her ring from park
ranger Marv Evans during
their wilderness wedding.
Afterward, the couple
leads off a spirited Virginia
reel. Guests hiked or rode
horseback to the ceremony,
held at Muir Trail Ranch
near the Pacific Crest
Trail and the South Fork
of the San Joaquin River.

*"Happiness and love in life
are what we wish for each other."*

Still laden with ice in mid-June, the sunset-tinted surface of the upper Rae Lake forms a textured pattern in blue-white and gold. Above, an example of glacial polish illustrates the effect of ice-age scouring on normally rough stone. Below, granite rocks lying in the shallows of Helen Lake, near Muir Pass, show in bright detail through 18 inches of the lake's clear, snow-fed waters.

Crouched in the shelter of a fallen pine near Palisade Lakes, a marmot peers out attentively as if deciding when to make its move. Always eager for a meal, these large rodents—some as long as 28 inches—scamper boldly into camp, rummage in packs if permitted, and carry off whatever tempts them. Equally at home in high altitudes but much more timid, a grouse perches on a branch, its mottled plumage blending with the shadowy forest behind it.

*"We camped with three chubby marmots
—waddling, inquisitive creatures."*

Massive shafts of basalt rise 60 feet high at Devils Postpile National Monument. The curious structure took shape about a million years ago when a deep pool of lava, cooling and hardening, cracked into angular columns. Glaciers later sheared off the top and side, leaving a rubble of broken pillars and an unfinished staircase for climbers. Here and there, wild flowers grow from niches in the weathered stone.

YOSEMITE, TAHOE, THE MOTHER LODE

4

MY FACE PRESSED HARD against the cold granite of a nearly vertical cliff as my weight rested precariously on a "flake"—a tiny ledge only half an inch wide. Slowly, deliberately, I moved my hand toward a vertical crack in the rock and stretched out my right leg, groping for another foothold. Feeling the reassuring tautness of the rope that was attached to my waist and anchored by a fellow climber at the top, I glanced again down the 60 feet of wall that I had already scaled and saw the jagged rocks at the bottom.

After a long step into space, my foot finally found another small flake. I jammed my hand into the crack, the most secure grip I'd had in ten minutes of climbing. The crack widened above my hand; pushing up from the flake, I lodged my left foot into the space, and easily scrambled the remaining 20 feet to the top of Puppy Dome.

There I joined the six other students taking a basic rock-climbing course with me in Yosemite National Park. Dave Bircheff, our wiry instructor, congratulated me on the climb, the culmination of a day-long class. From the clifftop I had a sweeping view of Tuolumne Meadows, a broad expanse of green cut by wandering streams. An imposing array of precipitous granite peaks and domes surrounded the Meadows, and I understood the enthusiasm of Loyd Price, chief guide of the Yosemite Mountaineering School: "We're spoiled here. There's no place in the world that has as much climbable rock in as concentrated an area with as much consistently good weather as Yosemite."

Dave, dressed in baggy knickers and a ragged white shirt, echoed Loyd's thoughts as we rested. "I've been climbing for 12 years"—he's only 26— "and what I like about Yosemite is that there's always another pitch that's a little more challenging than the last."

That night a storm front rolled across the sky, obliterating the stars, drenching and chilling the Meadows. An hour before dawn the raindrops were replaced by fat, wet snowflakes—in early July a surprise to the natives as well

Ignited by an abandoned campfire, a centuries-old Sierra juniper burns at dusk in the Desolation Wilderness, one of California's most heavily used wilderness areas. The random orange lines trace the paths of flying sparks.

as to me. I sat in a coffee shop with Doug most of the morning, waiting for a weak sun to melt the snow. Sam, hopscotching far north, was on a photographic expedition to Oregon's Mount Hood.

In early afternoon, Doug and I set out across the sodden Tuolumne Meadows, stopping at Soda Springs for a taste of the natural "quinine water" that bubbles from the ground. Early settlers exclaimed over the lightness of biscuits made with the water, and some backpackers we met had prepared an odd-tasting soft drink by sprinkling lemonade powder into the spring water.

The Tuolumne River curves through the Meadows for several miles before gathering speed and plunging over a series of cataracts. Paralleling the river, the trail crosses long tongues of bare granite, then drops into the spray of thundering Tuolumne Falls and the White Cascade. At Glen Aulin we turned north, and two miles up Cold Canyon we stopped for the night.

We had been warned by hikers and park rangers about the large population of bears in this area, and I recalled a report of John Muir's: "In my first interview with a Sierra bear we were frightened and embarrassed, both of us, but the bear's behavior was better than mine." We saw no sign of the animals, but as a safety precaution we placed our food in stuff sacks — the outer covers of our sleeping bags — and hung them, eight feet off the ground, from a rope slung between two trees a hundred feet from camp. Apparently the effort was unnecessary; the bags still hung unmolested in the morning, and we saw no tracks in the heavy frost.

Near the end of Cold Canyon we crossed a broad meadow where birds glided overhead and narrow streams laced the earth, and I thought about what I had learned of Sierra meadows. Glaciers, slowly grumbling down from the heights, had dredged hollows that became lakes as the ice retreated. Over the centuries, silt and rubble eroded from the mountains and filled the lakes; grass gradually took root, and the sweeping meadows of today were created. Now further change is overtaking them. I could see dozens of lodgepole pine seedlings encroaching at the edge of the meadow, the beginning of a process that one day will transform the meadow into forest.

Late in the afternoon I lay prone on a level rock, my chin resting on crossed hands, and gazed 500 feet down into Matterhorn Canyon. From this distant vantage I watched three miniature backpackers set up camp, gather wood, and start a small fire.

A 2,500-foot descent brought us from Benson Pass to Benson Lake the next morning. The trail edged through a flat, forested area that looked, from a ledge a hundred feet above, like solid ground; but in fact it was a swampy, mosquito-infested jungle. Almost immediately we lost the trail and started slogging across the boggy soil, stepping over moldering logs, avoiding pools of stagnant water. The air lay steamy and still, and insects hovered in swarms. For 20 minutes we stumbled through this morass before breaking into the open.

Our pleasure at reaching Grace Meadow, a mile-long band of green crossed by Falls Creek, was soon erased by the incessant whine of mosquitoes. In the first 50 yards they were merely annoying, but suddenly a black cloud whirled around my head and body. I flailed my arms, slapped my legs, swung my map like a fan; with each breath I was certain I had inhaled a couple of the hateful insects. I even tried to run from them, pack and all. Finally I reached the northern end of Grace Meadow and climbed out of their province. I paused to count the score: I had 16 welts on arms, legs, and face, but I reckoned I had killed at least 25 of the enemy.

Horses are permitted on the Pacific Crest—unlike the Appalachian Trail—but we had not encountered any horsemen until just north of Grace Meadow, when we met a mounted family of five accompanied by several pack animals. Although I enjoy horseback riding, joint use of a trail is not quite agreeable to either backpacker or horseman. The pounding of hooves leaves a thick layer of dust, and manure and flies pollute pathway and campsite alike. On the other hand, hikers with their bulky packs can cause a horse to shy or bolt. At least as far as the Pacific Crest Trail is concerned, I am prepared to invoke the wisdom of Thomas Jefferson: "Walking is the best possible exercise. Habituate yourself to walk very far. The Europeans value themselves on having subdued the horse to the uses of man; but I doubt whether we have not lost more than we have gained, by the use of this animal."

A morning's hike took us over Dorothy Lake Pass, at the northern border of Yosemite, to the West Fork of the West Walker River. As I dipped my cup into its swift, cold water, I glimpsed a flash of auburn on the opposite bank. It was a diminutive red fox, among the stealthiest of Sierra predators.

For the next several miles we followed the river, named for Joseph Reddeford Walker, one of the earliest explorers of these mountains. In November 1833, with a company of about 40 men, this rugged pioneer forced a westward crossing of the Sierra although the snows had drifted "from ten to one hundred feet deep." Following a branch of this same river, the determined trappers climbed for three weeks under extreme conditions; when their supply of jerked buffalo meat ran out, they had to kill horses to survive. Coming down the western slope, Walker made two of the most remarkable discoveries

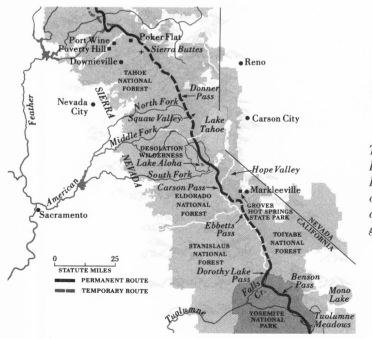

Along the Sierra crest, colorful place names stir memories of the past. The words *Yosemite, Toiyabe,* and *Tahoe* suggest their Indian origin. Farther north, *Port Wine, Poverty Hill,* and *Poker Flat* recall the time of the forty-niners. Today, tourists as well as persistent miners pan for gold in the Mother Lode country.

by an American trailblazer: Yosemite Valley and a grove of giant sequoias.

Continuing north, we crossed the path of the first white man known to have breached the Sierra Nevada, Jedediah Strong Smith. A grim, lean Yankee who always carried a rifle and a Bible, Smith gained early fame as a trapper, taking a record 668 beaver pelts in one season. In May 1827, after leading a party across the Mojave Desert to the Pacific Ocean, Smith and two comrades sought and found a route across the Sierra—possibly at Ebbetts Pass. In a letter to William Clark of the Lewis and Clark Expedition, Jed Smith tersely described his feat: ". . . started on the 20th of May, and succeeded in crossing it in eight days, having lost only two horses and one mule."

The next pass north from Ebbetts opened to the white man in the winter of 1844, when "the Pathfinder," John C. Frémont, penetrated from the east with two famous mountain men, Kit Carson and Tom (Broken Hand) Fitzpatrick. Pushing up the East Carson River, they encountered an old Indian who offered a dire warning: "Rock upon rock—rock upon rock—snow upon snow—snow upon snow. Even if you get over the snow you will not be able to get down from the mountain." Despite those grim words, the obstinate Frémont continued into the high country where a series of gales and snowstorms tested his men with fatigue, hunger, and snow blindness.

Finally, on February 6, Frémont with Carson and several companions climbed a peak from which they could see the Sacramento Valley and the distant skyline of the Coast Range; and eight days later the troop reached the Sierra crest at a point near Carson Pass. There were still the tedious trials of the descent, as the old Indian had foretold, and Frémont recorded that the route was "steep, and slippery with snow and ice, and the tough evergreens of the mountain impeded our way, tore our skins and exhausted our patience."

The first time I saw Carson Pass, the conditions were similar. Deep snow mantled the ground, and a piercing wind rustled through the contorted branches of juniper trees. It was still an hour before dawn, the air was biting cold, the sky was a swirling blue-gray. Sam and I had journeyed here in late winter to learn about another use of the Pacific Crest Trail—cross-country skiing. We enrolled in the Viggo Nordic Ski School in snowy Hope Valley, just east of Carson Pass. From the moment we arrived, we were enveloped by the warmth and helpfulness of the co-owners, Elena Vialo and Gunnar Vatvedt. Elena, of the musical laugh, is the hostess and gourmet cook; Norwegian-born Gunnar is the chief instructor.

In one day Gunnar taught Sam and me the basics of cross-country skiing. Sam, who had skied before, quickly overcame most of his rustiness. I, however, had never even stood on skis, and had trouble with balance as well as technique. In his heavy accent the tall, ruddy Gunnar constantly shouted encouragement: "Good, good. Much better. Relax in your knees; your legs are too tense. You want to flow over the ground." I gradually improved, but I never flowed.

Early the next morning I clipped long, tapered Nordic skis to my boots and began shuffling over the crusty snow. Sam, Gunnar, and I skirted a low meadow just north of Carson Pass and began to climb a ridge, generally following the route of the Pacific Crest Trail. When the slope became too steep for Sam and me on our skis, we balanced them on our shoulders and crunched our way to the top. Dawn was near and the wind whipped sharply on the ridgetop. Skis hissing on the powder snow, we dropped from the ridge hoping to rendezvous at Meiss Lake with another party from Gunnar's school.

We crossed the frozen lake in effortless style; with a strong wind at our backs, we simply held out our arms like sails and glided across the snow. We aimed for a mound of white that Gunnar said was a snow shelter, and a small bundled figure emerged: Pekka Poutanen, from Finland, one of Gunnar's ski instructors. He gave an enthusiastic report. "The snow is great — some of the best I've seen since leaving Finland. I've got seven high school students from San Francisco up here on a five-day ski-touring trip. We built this cave of snow blocks the first day, and since then we've spent almost every daylight hour out skiing." The hardy Pekka seemed to thrive on the harsh conditions of winter. So did the teen-agers I met inside, despite their complaints about cold and sunburn. They were just clambering out of their sleeping bags when Sam, Gunnar, and I entered, and they regaled us all through breakfast with tales of their adventures.

Gunnar crawled out of the shelter with a broad smile creasing his face. "When they talk like that, I feel happy. I like to see people come here and enjoy themselves in the midst of nature."

For several more hours we skied in the crisp, white winter landscape, but by midafternoon my ankles and leg muscles were crying for a break. We returned to the school, picked up Elena, and drove to nearby Grover Hot Springs State Park. A natural spring feeds a large pool, where I soaked languidly in the steamy 105° water for an hour. "You should be here when it's snowing," said Elena. "It's beautiful to lie back in the water and watch the flakes drift down and mingle with the mist."

That evening we sat on pillows around a remarkable table, a seven-foot cross section from a cedar trunk, and ate an unforgettable meal of fresh mushroom soup, salmon pie, watercress salad, strawberries and cream, sour cream cake, and white wine. Afterward, to combat my drowsiness from the strenuous day and the huge meal, I stepped outdoors into the cold night air. The stars were brilliant in a moonless sky. A cluster of skis sticking out of a snowbank reminded me of the stories I had read about the first man to ski these mountains, John A. (Snowshoe) Thompson.

In 1856 Thompson, an immigrant from Norway, volunteered to carry the mail in winter across the crest of the Sierra between Placerville, California, and Genoa, Nevada — a distance of 110 miles. From valley oak he crafted a pair of skis that measured ten feet long and six inches wide and weighed 25 pounds. For the next 20 winters he rode those massive skis over the high passes and through Hope Valley, carrying as much as 80 pounds of mail on his back and making the round trip in only five days. He always traveled alone, subsisting on dried beef and biscuits. Thompson took great pride in his work, and neither demanded nor received payment.

Before stepping back into the warmth of the dining room, I glanced toward snowbound Carson Pass and wondered, as Frémont had done, how summer would transform it. "Scenery and weather combined," he once wrote, "must render these mountains beautiful in summer."

He was right. In mid-July, when the trail brought me to Carson Pass, I found it was graced with warm breezes, billowing green grass, and gardens of wild flowers. Playful streams trickled down the ridge up which Gunnar, Sam, and I had trudged in deep snow. The flowing water nourished stands of lavender lupine, scarlet Indian paintbrush, and delicate red and yellow columbines. I paused for long minutes in the colorful glens, admiring the flowers and trying to picture the snows of winter. At the top of the treeless ridge I came upon an expanse of western irises. Atop the slender, two-foot stalks opened lovely blossoms, each displaying shades of purple, lavender, yellow, and white. The Greek word *iris* means "rainbow," and looking at the delicate interplay of colors within each flower, I could think of no more fitting name.

At the end of the ridge I looked north past Meiss Lake, now meadow-rimmed and sparkling, to a far larger expanse of blue. Mark Twain wrote of Lake Tahoe, "...I thought it must surely be the fairest picture the whole earth affords." Guarded by massive peaks, framed by stately conifers, Tahoe presents one of the most impressive scenes in the Sierra Nevada from the vantage of the Pacific Crest Trail, which winds high above its western shore.

For the first time since leaving Mexico, I was hiking alone for an extended period. Sam was still photographing Mount Hood, and Doug had flown home to Toledo for a week. I looked forward to the challenge of self-reliance and the rewards of individual accomplishment. I was aware of potential hazards, however, and carefully packed extra food and first-aid supplies.

Climbing above Echo Lakes, I entered Desolation Wilderness—an area that would later fascinate Doug and Sam—and a meandering forest walk brought me to broad Lake Aloha and Desolation Valley. The lake, dotted with hundreds of barren islets, partially fills a severe granite valley relieved only by a few scattered pines. The Crystal Range, tall and gray, backs the western shore. Stopping for lunch on a rock slab, I sat at the center of a stark domain of gray rock, blue water, and cloudless sky. From Aloha, I descended through snow banks to narrow Heather Lake and soon reached tree-lined Susie Lake. On a stony peninsula spiked by a single dead tree, I made camp, and spent an afternoon of solitude resting on the sun-warmed rocks, exploring the shoreline, swimming, and watching the play of the wind on the water. I thought on the pleasures of backpacking, and for the moment I was happy to be alone.

Heading north the next day, I overtook a group of teen-agers from Sacramento on a three-day hike. One 16-year-old boy, supported by two husky friends, was limping badly. "I was rock-climbing, and slipped on some moss," he said through clenched teeth. "I've either sprained or broken my ankle." I wrapped it with an extra elastic bandage, and left him some aspirin to dull the pain of hobbling the remaining few miles to a roadhead.

The trail took me through the mountains west of Lake Tahoe, past Squaw Valley—site of the 1960 Winter Olympics—to Donner Pass, where the ill-fated Donner Party suffered through the winter of 1846. By a combination of poor planning and bad luck, the train of 82 men, women, and children in 23 wagons reached the Sierra Nevada from the Midwest in October, after winter had set in. On November 1, the first wagons left Donner Lake for the 1,100-foot climb to the pass; they were soon floundering in five feet of snow and had to turn back. Snow and rain continued to fall, several subsequent attempts to walk or snowshoe across the pass failed, and food supplies dwindled.

On December 16, a group of 17 men and women set out with six days' rations in a futile attempt to cross the pass and reach the settlement of Bear Valley on the western slope. More than a month later, seven emaciated members of the party — including all five women — arrived at an Indian village. They had survived by eating the flesh of their dead comrades.

A rescue party reached the winter camp near the pass on February 18. They found a desperate group of starving people. For weeks the trapped emigrants had lived on a nauseating paste made by boiling cattle hides for hours; whenever someone died, the survivors resorted to cannibalism. Of the 82 who had reached the Sierra, only 47 lived through the ordeal, and many of these bore physical or mental scars for the rest of their lives.

Other dramatic history surrounds the Pacific Crest Trail as it winds through central California, which only a century and a quarter ago crawled with hordes of men seeking sudden wealth in gold. On January 24, 1848, James Marshall spotted flecks of yellow in the millrace of Sutter's Mill on the South Fork of the American River. In time his discovery captured the attention of the nation, and thousands of forty-niners swarmed to the Mother Lode.

North of Donner Pass, I hiked through land that once pulsed with mining activity, and came within a few miles of abandoned gold camps with names like Poverty Hill, Port Wine, and Poker Flat. In Downieville, a mining town that survives, I met a crusty 70-year-old prospector named Parley D. Vail.

"As a precaution against bears, we slung our food high between trees."

"I started prospecting in Montana in the '20's," P. D. told me, "and I ain't stopped yet." A toothless, heavy-set man in voluminous bib overalls, he drove me in a four-wheel-drive truck from Downieville to his 20-acre claim. At breakneck speed we bumped along the narrow rutted road above the Downie River; with a sweeping gesture that almost took us off the edge, P. D. said, "This country ain't even been scratched for gold yet. The forty-niners only got 10 to 15 percent of the gold, and that leaves a lot for me. Every storm and spring melt washes more gold down from the mountains; all you got to do is go out and work for it."

Before he took me to where he and his 31-year-old partner, Jerry Wesley, were currently working, we stopped at his shack while P. D. fixed himself breakfast on a wood-burning stove: four eggs, a quarter-pound of bacon, and a small mountain of toast. "You know, the best thing about mining is it's good exercise," he said, slapping butter and jam on the toast. "I'm going to keep at it as long as I can, and if I find a big strike, I may keep at it forever."

We walked up narrow Daves Creek, passing places that P. D. and Jerry had already worked. "That's the secret to this whole thing. You find a creek, you work it from the bottom to the top, you don't skip nothing. Right along there"—he pointed to a ledge with water gushing over it—"is where Jerry made our big find—a nugget that weighs nine ounces and is three inches by two. I thought the kid was going to drown when he first saw it."

A hundred yards farther we came upon Jerry, standing waist-deep in water, wearing a snorkel and mask, and working a dredger—a machine that vacuums the creek bottom, sucking rocks, gravel, sand, and sometimes gold into a sluice box. Dripping, Jerry climbed out of the creek and he and P. D. demonstrated the gold-panning art. They filled an 18-inch-wide, 3-inch-deep metal pan with material from the sluice box, then scooped in a little water. "Slosh it around at first to make the gold settle," Jerry said, "then begin slowly spilling out the water and rock."

With utmost care I followed his instructions, and after ten minutes I had cleared away most of the material. Picking out the last pebbles, I saw a gleam that has entranced thousands before me. Three tiny golden flakes rested in the bottom of the pan. In my excitement, I almost knocked it off my knees; Jerry picked the flakes out with tweezers and put them in a plastic vial. "Well, that'll pay for the day's gasoline," P. D. said with a smile.

Back in his truck, he rested his hands on the steering wheel and stared out the window. "I guess all I've ever really wanted out of life is to get by," he said. "But from time to time I wonder: What would have happened if I'd ever made that one big strike?"

Shadows move across the sheer face of El Capitan as two expert rock-climbers, midway through their four-day ascent, prepare to bivouac in hammocks. The granite monolith rises 3,614 feet above Yosemite Valley.

ABOVE: WILD COLUMBINE

Dawn finds a cross-country skier on the wind-sculptured ridge of Elephants Back.

The varied terrain of California's high country draws both novice and advanced trail skiers.

In the dining room of the Viggo Nordic Ski School, co-owners Elena Vialo and Gunnar Vatvedt talk with Will about the satisfactions of exploring the wilderness in wintertime. The school teaches cross-country skiing techniques and organizes snow-camping trips. To rendezvous with one group of campers, Will, Sam, and Gunnar skied the Pacific Crest Trail from the school's headquarters near Carson Pass to Meiss Lake. There they visit (opposite) with three of Gunnar's students in a tarp-covered snow cave, base for day-touring among the rugged peaks and high valleys of the Sierra.

DOUG GOSLING

Amid an expanse of bare granite in the Desolation Wilderness, a hiker
watches the path of the moon's reflection on Lake Aloha. Above its banks
Doug Gosling stretches out on a ledge polished by glaciers 100,000 years ago.
After the great rivers of ice had gouged hollows in the bedrock and then
retreated, snowmelt and rainwater formed clear, still pools. The surface of
one of these (above) perfectly reflects a rocky wall, and Sam later discovered
—in turning the photograph sideways—a symmetrical and grotesque face.

With water pumped from a nearby stream,
a Forest Service fire fighter douses a blaze
near the trail; his hose snakes across charred
ground cover. Pausing to wipe ashes from his
eye, line boss Mark Smith names the culprit:
"A careless camper—the cause of 75 percent of
the fires we fight in the Desolation Wilderness."

*"This country ain't even
been scratched for gold yet.
All you got to do is
go out and work for it."*

*Prospector P. D. Vail, mining his 20-acre claim along Daves Creek, totes
a heavy pan of stream-bed gravel — and maybe some gold. At his cabin
near Downieville, P. D. assures visitors that the Mother Lode country
still holds plenty of mineral wealth. His claim, first mined by forty-
niners, yields gold dust, flakes, and an occasional nugget.*

FROM LASSEN'S FIRES
TO THE COAST RANGE

5

"LIGHTNING makes an incredible whipping and cracking sound just before it hits. Then there's a loud buzzing like radio static as the thunderclap shakes the whole building. Sometimes there's a blue glow around the roof overhang, and I've even seen electricity arc back and forth between the beams. The first time I saw that, man, I was scared!"

Bill Thomason sat with his feet on a desk inside the fire lookout station that perches — at 8,587 feet — atop the highest of the Sierra Buttes. The thumb-like spires of volcanic rock provide a vantage high above the rolling ridges of the northern Sierra, and I could trace, far below, the Pacific Crest Trail near Sardine Lakes. A side trail ended at the base of the 178 metal steps that climbed the rocks to our steel-and-glass cage.

Bill, a college student who works summers as a fire guard for the U. S. Forest Service, continued to describe the awesome display of a thunderstorm, and I was glad that the sky was bright blue and cloudless. "One of the first things I learned," Bill said, "was not to touch metal during electrical storms. But I've gotten so used to them now that I can usually sleep right through."

What were his duties? "Basically, I just look for smoke. After a while you get to know the country so well that anything out of the ordinary pops right out.

"When I sight a column of smoke, I take a compass reading and check my card file to see if it's coming from a sawmill, say, or a campground. If not, I radio headquarters to have it checked out. Fortunately, this area's not too vulnerable; there are relatively few fires each year."

I asked Bill whether the isolation of sitting alone high on a remote mountain ever bothered him. "Usually it's not all that lonely," he answered. "Besides the hiking path, there's a jeep trail, so I get a few visitors almost every day. Sometimes more than a few — over the Fourth of July weekend, at least 150 people trooped through. And there's always communication through the radio. But I have gone as long as four days without seeing anyone. I guess

Thermal mudpots, dry at the moment, periodically bubble with liquid mud at the edge of Boiling Springs Lake in Lassen Volcanic National Park. Steam from underground heats the mud to boiling and the lake water to 125°.

I've learned to appreciate both company and loneliness. The time of day I most like to be alone is at sunset. It's so peaceful up here then."

A dozen miles north of Sierra Buttes, the trail skirts placid Gold Lake, named in acknowledgment of one of the biggest hoaxes of the gold rush days. In 1849 vague rumors of a lake with banks strewn with gold spread through the mining camps. In the early summer of 1850, an English miner named J. R. Stoddard appeared in Nevada City with a poke of nuggets and a dramatic tale. While on a hunting trip, he said, he had stumbled on the fabled lake of gold, and was astounded by its abundance of riches. As he scooped up hand-fuls of nuggets, he was suddenly attacked by Indians, and was wounded in the leg by an arrow while escaping.

He offered—for a price—to lead an expedition back to the lake; dozens of gold-hungry prospectors responded and paid the fee. When the party left Nevada City, a throng of perhaps a thousand other men followed along.

For days the horde vainly tramped the mountains. Stoddard became increasingly vague about his bearings, until at last the miners rebelled and gave him an ultimatum: He had 24 hours to find the lake or he would be strung from the nearest tree.

That night the wily Stoddard stole out of camp and disappeared. In the morning the miners, thoroughly chagrined, headed back to their old claims or sought new ones in the Gold Lake country.

Sam and Doug, back from their separate trips, rejoined me on the trail north of Gold Lake and together we walked the dry, hot ridges of the northern Sierra. Late one afternoon, as we followed a dusty road toward a bluff over-looking the North Fork of the Feather River, the aroma of cooking drew us toward a small prefabricated house alive with young men.

It was a crew of the California Ecology Corps, sponsored by the California Division of Forestry. Under contract with the U. S. Forest Service, the men were building a six-mile section of Pacific Crest Trail from the ridgetop down into the Feather River Canyon near the town of Belden. After we had de-molished a supper of roast beef and corn on the cob, I sat sipping coffee and talking to Dick Hansen, project foreman and a 20-year veteran of the Division of Forestry, and Rick Lawrence, the 22-year-old crew leader.

"We've been up here for just under three weeks, and we've already got more than half a mile of trail built," Dick said with pride. "The whole project should take no more than four or five months, we hope."

"We're averaging about 250 feet of finished trail per day," Rick added, "and that's through manzanita, which is hard to dig out. We have to follow strict specifications of trail width and drainage, of course, and we're anxious to do a good job; we're hoping that this one will lead to more contracts."

I asked about the young men comprising the Ecology Corps. "They're mostly in their late teens or early twenties," Rick answered. "Some are high school drop-outs, others are working during summer vacation from college, some are just rootless right now. The corps is a good place for a guy to do some hard work, earn a little money, and sort out his thoughts and his objectives.

"As for myself, I'm working for college credit. This assignment is part of a director-leadership course for a bachelor's degree in the field of parks and recreation. It's also great practical experience."

In the late mountain twilight the corpsmen returned from swimming, fishing, or rock climbing and crawled into the sleeping bags scattered around the prefab building. A few minutes after five o'clock the next morning I was served a tasty cheese and mushroom omelet by camp cook Jim Atha. Breakfast over, we crowded into a truck and bumped along the dirt road leading to the new trail site.

Following the newly constructed section, I rounded a well-engineered switchback and faced a tangle of brush. Ahead of me a proficient team of two strong corpsmen worked with lopping shears to cut out the tough branches and trunks and form a rough corridor. A couple of dozen yards behind them, another team wielding picks and shovels grubbed out rocks and roots and widened the initial path. Other teams graded, cleared, and trimmed, until finally a permanent section of Pacific Crest Trail had been completed.

"We rotate the men every day so they don't get burned out on any one job," Rick told me. "As we work, we're careful to preserve the natural lay of the land as much as possible. We only take out boulders or trees where they would be a serious hindrance to hikers."

From the top of the canyon wall, Rick looked down at his crew and said, "This is the kind of work you can appreciate doing. You feel like you're leaving your mark, that you can come back in 20 years and be proud of what you've accomplished."

Beyond the Feather River, the trail crawls along the northernmost slopes

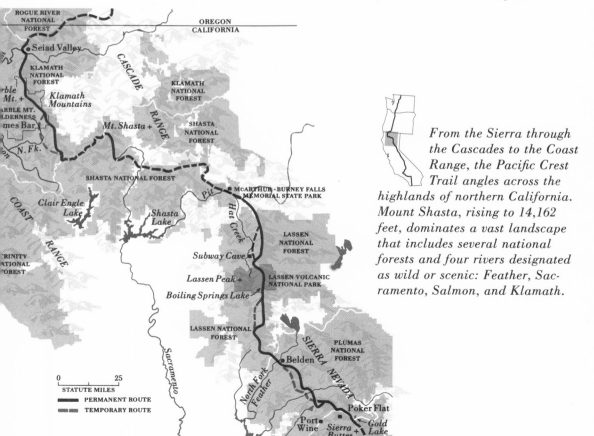

From the Sierra through the Cascades to the Coast Range, the Pacific Crest Trail angles across the highlands of northern California. Mount Shasta, rising to 14,162 feet, dominates a vast landscape that includes several national forests and four rivers designated as wild or scenic: Feather, Sacramento, Salmon, and Klamath.

of the Sierra Nevada and enters the realm of the Cascade Range, which extends from northern California through Oregon and Washington and into Canada. The low, furrowed ridges of the Cascades are punctuated by jutting cones of dormant volcanoes. These glacier-clad giants, rising thousands of feet above the surrounding countryside, are among the most dramatic and graceful mountains along the trail. From Lassen Peak to Glacier Peak, their crowns make singular trail markers.

Southernmost of the cones is 10,457-foot Lassen, focal point of Lassen Volcanic National Park and the only active volcano within the continental United States.

Between 1914 and 1917, Lassen Peak growled and grumbled, spewed steam and lava, and produced earth tremors, mudflows, and billowing clouds of cinders. The most frightening eruption occurred on May 22, 1915, when a massive explosion rocked the region, created a mushroom-shaped cloud of steam and ashes that rose to 30,000 feet, and sent an avalanche of lava surging down Lassen's northeast slope.

Evidence that Lassen's fires are not yet completely banked awaited us at Boiling Springs Lake, just within the national park boundary. From a low ridge, the trail winds through a dry pine forest; the first indication that Sam, Doug, and I had of the lake's existence was a sulphurous odor that grew steadily stronger. We soon came to the treeline and saw a steaming, milky green pond ringed by cracked gray mud. The lake's turbid waters are heated to 125° by steam rising through underground fissures. At the edge of the lake the steam has created mudpots, cavities containing viscous mud through which hot vapors belch and gurgle.

The bizarre sights, sounds, and smells of Boiling Springs Lake form a sensory fantasyland that held us for more than an hour. As we were shouldering our packs to leave, we heard a shout and turned to see a trio of hikers hurrying toward us. As they approached we recognized Denise Myers, Hal Simmons, and Robert Clancy, hikers from Colorado whom we had encountered on the trail before, and who had undertaken to hike the entire Pacific Crest Trail in one summer.

Seeing their familiar smiles reminded me of something I had learned during my first few weeks of hiking: It's hard to remain a stranger on the trail. Conversation and good fellowship come easy, and backpackers share an awareness of mutual dependence. I knew that if an accident befell me, I could count on help from almost any fellow hiker.

After exchanging news of recent weeks, we agreed to hike together for a couple of days through Lassen Park. Under menacing clouds, Hal, Denise, and I continued down the trail while the other three lingered at Boiling Springs Lake, Sam and Clancy to photograph and Doug to wander into nearby meadows and study the flora. Doug's interest in plants never flagged, and he passed his enthusiasm to others.

We came to sloping Warner Valley, and crossed Hot Springs Creek just as a thunderstorm broke. Taking refuge in a dense copse of pines, we talked while the rain drummed down. I asked Hal and Denise about some of the results of their months of hiking. "Well," began Hal, a bronzed man of 25 with a bushy brown beard, "I've learned a lot about myself, and I've begun to sort my life out—determine what I'm good at and what I want to do in the future. Spending this summer hiking has given new direction to my life."

Denise, slight and lithe with sandy hair and a smattering of freckles, said, "As you walk, your mind has so much time to think that you can really analyze situations and find solutions. I think I've figured out my relationships with other people—with all my friends and relatives at home."

"We've learned more than ever the value of friendship," Hal continued, "especially through the people we've met in small towns. Some of them have been wonderful—there've been postmasters who have opened up their post offices at night so we could get our food packages, people who have taken us in as houseguests, people who have given us a roof in bad weather."

"We always try to return their kindness," Denise said, "even if it's just weeding their garden or helping with some other chore. After an experience like that, I feel that everyone has benefited."

As we talked, the thunderstorm reached a crescendo and then began to fade. A few rays of sunlight broke through the clouds and transformed raindrops on pine needles into sparkling jewels. Suddenly two young deer bounded through the high grass with long, graceful leaps.

Camped that evening on a knoll above Warner Valley, we lounged around the fire watching Clancy make bread. To a packaged biscuit mix he added oats, brown sugar, and water, then sprinkled in nuts, raisins, and finely sliced orange peel, and buried the covered pot in the red-hot coals. An hour later he brought forth his specialty—dense, moist, and delicious.

For the next couple of days we hiked slowly, swimming in lakes, taking cover during thunderstorms, and talking late each evening. We came to the boundary of the park at noon on a hot day, and decided to have a last lunch together before Hal, Denise, and Clancy resumed a demanding schedule that averaged 17 miles per hiking day. We lingered over the meal, but soon our trio of ambitious hikers packed up and disappeared to the north.

We followed at a slower pace, paralleling Hat Creek and dodging between large expanses of lava. In the jumble of black volcanic matter called the Devils Half Acre, we explored Subway Cave. Here about 2,000 years ago a fresh lava flow began to cool and harden on the outside while the molten interior continued to ooze downhill, leaving a hollow cave or lava tube. With flashlights and jackets, Sam, Doug, and I ventured into the quarter-mile-long passage and were quickly enveloped in the cool, silent darkness. The walls, floor, and ceiling were surprisingly smooth, and we switched off our lights and groped our way into a large chamber called the Sanctum, where the blackness seemed absolute.

Back on Hat Creek, we rounded a bend and saw—still 75 miles away— the soaring, snow-mantled form of Mount Shasta. "Lonely as God and white as a winter moon," poet Joaquin Miller described it. At 14,162 feet, this massive pyramid rises 10,000 feet above the surrounding terrain, and its glaciered heights would be visible to us at various points for the next 350 meandering miles of the trail.

While still some distance southeast of Shasta, we entered McArthur - Burney Falls Memorial State Park. With dozens of other tourists I took a nature trail to the base of slender, 129-foot-high Burney Falls, where I stood in cool spray at the edge of an emerald pool, hoping to spot one of the black swifts—the small, dark sea birds that make summer homes in the basalt cliff behind the falls. Suddenly I saw a flash of black and watched as one of the birds darted downstream on long, slender wings.

Following dirt roads, our route wound north and then west over low, dry ridges to a bridge crossing of the Sacramento River. In this area, the two great mountain systems of California merge: The Sierra Nevada - Cascade chain on the east and the Coast Range on the west bend toward each other and mingle into one broad band of highlands. Seeking the loftiest route, the Pacific Crest Trail swings west into the Coast Range, traversing the Klamaths and the Siskiyous and approaching within 50 miles of the Pacific Ocean, before circling east again to the Cascades in southern Oregon.

Two days of hiking took us well into the Klamaths, and one night we camped in the shelter of a splendid specimen of the sugar pine, tallest pine species in America, capable of growing to 200 feet. Scattered about the tree were dozens of its mammoth cones. Several measured 17 inches in length, and despite the sharp scales, Sam and I played a game of football with one. Later I learned that the sugar pine cones we found were only average; some grow as long as 23 inches.

"A high-rise apartment house for great blue herons..."

We followed the trail route to the forested banks of the North Fork of the Salmon River, where we sat quietly and stared into the quiet green pools, hoping to glimpse a salmon. As a schoolboy, I had learned that in late summer and early fall Pacific salmon leave their ocean habitat and swim up such freshwater streams to spawn and then to die. On a family trip to British Columbia when I was seven years old, I had seen salmon by the score — pink, wasted, and near death — splashing feebly in the shallow water of a stream after spawning.

Those reminiscences sparked an interest that I decided to pursue, so I left the trail and caught a ride to follow the Salmon River downstream to its junction with the mighty Klamath River. In the nearby village of Somes Bar, I met Willis Conrad, a short, muscular Karok Indian with a shock of black hair. We walked to a bluff high above the Klamath where it cascades over Ishi Pishi Falls.

"This has been a tribal fishing ground for centuries," Willis told me. "And it's protected by law for our use because it's ceremonial land. We're the only ones who can fish here, and we use only the traditional ways."

Willis offered to show me his tribe's method of fishing, and we scrambled down the bluff. Swirling water whipped to white froth tumbled down the cataract of Ishi Pishi Falls. Plumes of spray enfolded us and washed the rocks on which we carefully crossed. From behind a great boulder, Willis extracted a strange apparatus. Two slim, straight pieces of wood about 12 feet long formed a large V; a third piece of wood had been bowed to connect the arms at the wide end, completing a frame for a net. "We use strong fir for the poles of these dip nets," Willis said. "The bent wood is live oak — it's flexible when green, but very strong when it dries."

To the bowed section he tied a handmade net to form a mesh cup five feet deep and three feet across. "In the old days they used grass for the nets," he said, "but we use twine or nylon cord now. Over the years, people have tried different kinds of modern fishing equipment, but in the white water of these falls, only the traditional nets like this one really work."

How long had he been dipping for salmon? "Well, you kind of grow up with it," he answered. "I started when I was about 11, and I gradually caught on. It takes experience to be good at it, and it takes strength, too."

He stepped to a rock that protruded only a few inches above rushing water. Grasping one fir pole in each hand, he lowered the net into the river. "You can't see the fish," he called over the noise of the falls, "so you have to do everything by feel."

After five minutes of probing, his muscles suddenly tensed and he pulled the net up and out of the water. Thrashing wildly in the mesh was a three-foot-long, silvery gray Chinook salmon. A young Indian man who had been standing nearby walked over and clubbed the fish, and Willis dumped it out on the rocks. "I guess this one weighs about 30 pounds," he said. "Small compared to some. I caught one that weighed nearly 70 pounds. And when the salmon are really running, it's not unusual to catch several in the same dip. Once I had 11, and none of them weighed less than 20 pounds."

As Willis cleaned the fish, I asked how his wife would prepare it. "She will put up the meat in glass jars, and then cook it for four hours in its own juices," he said. "Florence counts on canning some salmon every year—we have five children."

Was Willis teaching any of them to dip-fish? "My boy is only in kindergarten, but I think I'll start teaching him one of these days. There are several young fellows who are learning right now. We're passing our traditions along."

Retracing my route up the Salmon River, I returned to the Pacific Crest Trail near the southern portal of Marble Mountain Wilderness. The trail wanders through this rugged country for more than 40 miles, twisting and turning up narrow river valleys and climbing high, wooded ridges. Marble Mountain contrasts vividly with the green forests: A great white giant whose top is solid limestone, it appears from a distance to wear a thick cap of snow.

Dropping out of the wilderness, the trail crosses the Klamath River near the village of Seiad Valley, last trailside settlement in California. In this town of a hundred people we met a gentle, elderly man named Clyde (Gramps) Ashinhurst, who told us about a logbook kept at the grocery store; it records news and reflections of long-distance hikers. "You backpackers are such nice people," he said, "and everyone has such interesting stories to tell. I love to sit down and chat with the hikers."

I paged through the log, reading the comments of others. Skip Drew, whom we had met in the Mojave Desert, wrote of a chance encounter he had with a mountain lion in the Sierra, and then concluded his letter: "This has been the best year of my life!"

But another hiker declared: "It's been a long hike and I'm glad to quit."

Denise Myers, one of our Colorado friends, was more philosophical: "We've learned so much we should receive a diploma at the end."

Late in the day, I wandered up the Klamath River, quietly observing slender, long-billed great blue herons as they waded, fished, or stood motionless in the rushing water. At one point I glanced up into a tall tree and saw half a dozen large nests on successively higher limbs. Several herons crouched in the nests or perched on nearby branches; the effect was of a high-rise apartment house designed especially for herons.

On a slab of rock surrounded by the waters of the Klamath, I sat watching the shadows of afternoon lengthen into evening. The only motion in the sky was that of a solitary golden eagle drifting on widespread wings. For several minutes it plied the air currents high above me before soaring out of view. Here, at the end of my journey through California, I saw in that graceful flight a reflection of the freedom I, too, had found.

In a journal maintained by the townspeople of Seiad Valley, Skip Drew reads comments of trail travelers. During a memorable summer, Skip and two companions hiked the Pacific Crest the length of California.

ABOVE: SUGAR PINE CONE

Muscles straining, workers of the California Ecology Corps cut through stubborn brush to clear a new section of the Pacific Crest Trail. The corps, sponsored by the California Division of Forestry, won contracts to build 32 miles of trail in the Sierra Nevada. Below, corpsmen look across an expanse of chaparral in the Feather River Canyon before starting to carve out the route selected by the U.S. Forest Service.

Expertly balancing his net beside Ishi Pishi Falls, a Karok Indian stands poised to dip

for salmon struggling up the Klamath River to spawn.

OREGON:
"GRATEFUL TO THE EYE"

6

DROWSING IN THE SADDLE on a bright June day in 1853, a young prospector named John Wesley Hillman rode up the conifer-studded flank of a mountain in southern Oregon. Suddenly his mule jerked to a halt, almost pitching him down a steep thousand-foot slope. As he recovered his balance, Hillman focused on an astonishing scene: a sparkling, incredibly blue lake extending six miles by four within a great stone bowl.

Overwhelmed by the grandeur before him, Hillman resorted to the obvious and named his discovery Deep Blue Lake. Sixteen years later the name was changed to Crater Lake, to indicate the mountain's volcanic origin.

Sam and I were already anticipating our first glimpse of Crater Lake when, 50 miles to the south, we began our hike through Oregon on the shore of Lake of the Woods, one of the Sky Lakes—a series of jewel-like pools strewn through a forest of hemlock and pine.

Those first days in Oregon were a surprise. For me, the state's name had always evoked images of cool green forests, alpine lakes, monumental peaks, and grassy meadows crossed by mountain streams. But here in southern Oregon we found the low, wooded ridges hot, dry, and dusty, a condition aggravated by the previous winter's subnormal snowfall and the tardiness of summer rains. Water was hard to come by, and we had to plan carefully from lake to lake. In late afternoon we reached the head of Long Lake, a narrow band of water cutting through the trees. We promptly stripped for a swim, and the thick, cool mud on the bottom felt as good to my feet as the bracing water did to the rest of my body.

While cooking supper, I glanced into a darkening meadow and was startled to see a prehistoric monster lurking there. The trunk and roots of a fallen tree, bleached by the sun and broken by time, had formed a convincing image of a dragon rising on its front feet, gnarled head erect.

Dawn brought a company of the Oregon legion of campsite robbers, tiny

Cook for an ice-climbing class on Mount Hood, Wendy Friedlander primes a kitchen lantern. The tent's snow floor, protected from the sun, had become a platform as the surrounding snowfield melted and settled.

gray birds masked with black hoods. Unimpressed with us, they hopped boldly past to reconnoiter our camp. Because of the distinctive marking, Sam dubbed them executioner birds, a tag we continued to use even after we learned the proper name: Oregon juncos.

For five days we made our leisurely way through the Sky Lakes. One afternoon we struggled to the top of Devils Peak, a 7,582-foot crag of crumbly volcanic rock. The climb took us above the pines for the first time in several days. From the trail crest we looked south to where Mount Shasta reared skyward through thin mist like an iceberg at sea; then north, where our way led to the walls of Crater Lake and beyond to Mount Thielsen. Scrambling down Devils Peak, we entered the Seven Lakes Basin.

Commanding a knoll in the basin is Honeymoon Cabin, a one-room log structure that houses the backcountry ranger. As Sam and I topped the hill, a great commotion of barking stopped us short. Two woolly white dogs charged toward us, but their tails signaled their friendly intent.

Out of the cabin hurried a young man with brown hair and a thick mustache. "Niki, Mishka, come here!" he called, then added to us, "We don't get many visitors here." As the handsome Samoyeds pranced in front of the cabin, summer ranger Art Callan invited us inside where his slim blond wife, Nancy, was boiling water for coffee. A roughhewn table, a potbellied stove, and a set of bunks comprised the cabin's furniture.

Nancy explained that she could only spend weekends with Art. "We're both working for our doctorates, mine in horticulture, Art's in botany," she said, "and being out here is a great practical experience. But I work as a research assistant in Medford, so I hike in 3½ miles from the nearest road on Friday evening and then go out again on Sunday."

The Sky Lakes area is under study for possible inclusion in the wilderness system. "I hope it's approved," Art said. "Nancy and I would like to think that future generations will be able to enjoy this area much as it is now." But even if it is designated wilderness, Art worries about the problem of human impact. "Trail use is growing every year, and already some of the major campgrounds are being trampled down. Part of the remedy, I hope, lies in the dedication of the individual ranger and the education of the individual hiker. People will have to want—and work—to keep our wildernesses from becoming wastelands."

Niki and Mishka chased after Sam and me for a hundred yards or so as we walked away from the cabin. The trail took us up the mountain called Big Bunchgrass and past a trio of cinder cones—Maude, Ethel, and Ruth—before leading into the so-called Oregon Desert.

A curious remnant of the volcanism that produced Crater Lake, the Oregon Desert is a tract of pumice and cinders covering several square miles. Only lodgepole pines, sturdy pioneer trees, have gained a foothold in the inhospitable soil. Above our heads they spread long green branches, but underfoot the desert lived up to its name. The earth was brown and cracked, sparsely scattered with pine needles and cones. Neither grass nor shrub relieved the stark landscape; no stream of water freshened the dry ground.

In the middle of this desert Sam and I stopped to rest. The parched earth seemed to creak as I set my pack down, and I felt waves of heat from both the sun and the ground.

Suddenly in the distance I heard a sound like the beating of large wings. It drew closer, high in the branches of the lodgepoles. Then a breath of air touched my face, and as rapidly faded; the sound murmured slowly away. In the stillness of the Oregon Desert I had briefly encountered the wind—surely the only moving thing for miles around—and I remembered a fragment from William Cullen Bryant: "A breeze came wandering from the sky, Light as the whispers of a dream."

In the half-light of evening we reached wispy Stuart Falls, at the southern

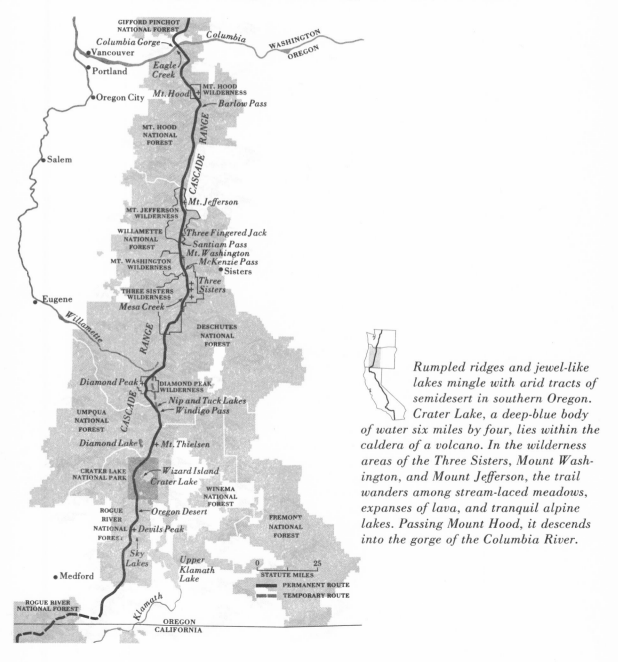

Rumpled ridges and jewel-like lakes mingle with arid tracts of semidesert in southern Oregon. Crater Lake, a deep-blue body of water six miles by four, lies within the caldera of a volcano. In the wilderness areas of the Three Sisters, Mount Washington, and Mount Jefferson, the trail wanders among stream-laced meadows, expanses of lava, and tranquil alpine lakes. Passing Mount Hood, it descends into the gorge of the Columbia River.

border of Crater Lake National Park—and here I forgot an important lesson learned much earlier. Overheated and thirsty, I sat down near the falls and drank several cups of water. The rapidly cooling air, the cold water, and a slight breeze coursing down the creek quickly conspired to chill me, and with a shiver I felt the first faint touch of hypothermia—the rapid loss of body heat that, unarrested, can kill. To combat it I quickly put on warm clothing and boiled water for a cup of bouillon.

That night, snug in my sleeping bag, I lay at the center of a ring of pines whose trunks soared skyward like the columns of a Greek ruin. Their crowns isolated a circular section of sky and focused my vision on individual stars—and then the stars became dreams.

Crater Lake! It was my first thought when I awoke, and after a hot, uphill hike on dusty fire roads, Sam and I finally reached the crater rim—and were as moved by the beauty of the scene as John Wesley Hillman had been. On all sides precipitous cliffs plunged into the dark blue water, from which the cinder cone called Wizard Island rose like a fairy-tale castle.

With only a raucous parade of large, sharp-beaked Clark's nutcrackers to distract us, we watched through the day as shifting sunlight changed the mood of the lake: fragile shadings in the morning, harsh at noon, mystical in the evening. At twilight a slowly deepening indigo transformed the crater yet again, and I understood why the Indians lived in such awe of the place.

Klamath legend tells of a fierce battle that raged between the Chief of the World Below, who commanded Mount Mazama—the mountain that would collapse to form the present caldera, or basin—and the Chief of the World Above, who fought from Mount Shasta. The dispute was over a Klamath maiden, and the two chiefs fought with molten rocks, hot ashes, and fire. Hoping to appease them, two Klamath medicine men sacrificed themselves in the caldron of Mount Mazama. Impressed by their bravery, the Chief of the World Above gave the earth a mighty shake, causing the top of Mazama to crash in on the Chief of the World Below; then he sent torrents of rain to fill the caldera.

"I guess there's really no such thing as a dead volcano," said Bruce Kaye, the tall park naturalist who had offered to drive Sam and me around Crater Lake's rim. Now, on a windswept crag called Discovery Point, we stood near the spot where Hillman first came upon the lake.

"The volcano we now call Mazama—the word means 'mountain goat' in Spanish—began forming one to two million years ago," said Bruce. "It gradually grew to a height of about 12,000 feet.

"But then, about 6,600 years ago, it destroyed itself. A vast reservoir of molten material under tremendous pressure from gases lay beneath the mountain. I compare it to a champagne bottle: When the cork is eased out, pressure is relieved, and gas and foam come rushing out. Well, a similar thing happened to Mazama. The volcanic gases began to escape, and pushed out the molten material—fiery lava and light, frothy pumice.

"These violent eruptions left a huge subterranean cavern that couldn't support the weight of the fractured mountain. Finally it just collapsed; the mountain fell in on itself, and the top 6,000 feet of Mazama was gone, leaving the great caldera that now holds the lake. But the volcanic activity wasn't over: Wizard Island, a volcano within a volcano, was built up by subsequent eruptions. Then, less than two thousand years ago, rainwater and melting snow began to fill the basin and form the lake. Its depth has stabilized at an average 1,932 feet, since the annual precipitation is balanced by evaporation and seepage."

With Bruce at the wheel, we continued on the Rim Drive, a spectacular 33-mile loop. Sam asked Bruce if he had ever hiked all the way around the lake. "No," was the reply, "but I like to bicycle around it. And in the winter some people circle it on snowshoes or cross-country skis."

The thought of a bicycle came temptingly to mind early the next morning as Sam and I left Crater Lake for Mount Thielsen, core of a volcano even older than Mazama. Named for Hans Thielsen, Danish-born civil engineer who developed many of Oregon's railroads, it juts above Diamond Lake to an elevation of 9,182 feet.

A spine of rock thrusting westward from Thielsen overlooked Diamond Lake and the forested country rolling north toward the peaks called the Three Sisters. Behind us, muted hues of gray, ocher, and russet tinted the rock walls and talus of Mount Thielsen. Because of the view, and despite a strong wind that blew across the exposed ridge, we decided to camp here, and quickly put up a foot-high wall of rocks as a windbreak. During the night I woke periodically to watch an almost-full moon trace its arc across the sky; near dawn it seemed to halt in place and hang, poised, a blood-red orb on the western horizon.

The wind chased us from the ridge early. We packed up, scattered our windbreak, and walked the two downhill miles to Thielsen Creek. We planned to have a quick breakfast, fill our water containers, and push on, but the sight of running water and green grass enticed us to linger and explore the creek. Once, stooping for a drink, I was surprised to see a small rock float by. As I watched, others bobbed past, ranging in size from a large pea to a pincushion. I fished several out and found them to be pieces of featherweight pumice.

A 12-mile walk brought us to a small clearing on a ridge of Tolo Mountain. The maps had indicated water here, but we found only a small puddle at the bottom of a 500-foot bluff. Sliding down proved easy; trudging back up, with pans of water in hand, was exhausting. But a reward came at dusk, when the full moon rose in the east to mirror the setting sun in the west.

The next day was a scorcher. We had set out with only half a bottle of water, since neither Sam nor I relished the thought of a morning descent of that slope to draw more. The bottle was almost empty when we reached Windigo Pass at noon, and the nearest fresh water was at Nip and Tuck Lakes, more than two miles away.

During the endless hike there, my thoughts centered on only one thing: water. As I became increasingly dehydrated, I felt a twinge of stomach cramps, and became slightly dizzy. My throat was so dry that my tongue stuck to the roof of my mouth. The infrequent sips that Sam and I allotted ourselves helped for only a few seconds; even resting was unsatisfactory, just a further delay in reaching our goal. I reflected that we had crossed the sun-baked Mojave Desert with relative ease, and now here, in what I had pictured as a land of flowing streams, I was suffering from severe thirst.

Finally, when I was beginning to wonder if we had somehow missed them, Nip and Tuck Lakes came into view. The tepid lake water and a chaser of tart lemonade revived me, and a swim followed by a three-hour nap brought me back to good spirits. But those spirits were tempered with new wisdom: I vowed never again to be caught short of water while backpacking.

Just south of the Three Sisters one sultry afternoon, I saw something glinting black in the dust underfoot. It turned out to be a puzzle—an arrowhead-like point, chipped from shiny obsidian, but too concave to be serviceable. I kept it as a souvenir, and I still try to imagine who made it and when, and how it ended up partially buried in the middle of the Pacific Crest Trail.

Gusty rain squalls, our first wet weather in Oregon, struck the day before we reached the glacier-clad Three Sisters. Pine needles drifted in pools of water as we set up the tent in a small clearing near the trail.

While the sun was drying our gear next morning, down the trail came a man bent nearly double by the enormous load on his back. Strapped to his pack was a large cardboard box, with shovels and axes laced to its sides. He reminded me of an ant carrying a massive bread crumb.

Backing up to a tree, he rested his burden on a branch to relieve some of the weight. "I don't dare sit down," he gasped. "If I did, I'd never get up." He glanced around our camp. "You're lucky you weren't here early yesterday afternoon," he said. "Lightning hit in several places, and started two small fires a mile north, but we parachuted in and got to them before they spread. The others are still keeping an eye on them."

He introduced himself as James Lawson, a smoke jumper for the Forest Service. "I love my job, but it's a lot easier jumping in with this stuff than packing it out. I've got parachutes, tents, garbage, all kinds of stuff—I figure it weighs about 120 pounds." He moved off with a brisk but wobbly gait.

At the southern portal of the Three Sisters chain lies Sisters Mirror Lake, which catches the reflection of the top of South Sister—at 10,358 feet the highest of the three peaks. Stretched out on a rock at the lake's edge to study a map, I learned that the Three Sisters—South, Middle, and North—are not the whole family. Neighboring peaks bear the names of The Wife, The Husband, and Little Brother. Rising above Sisters Mirror Lake is The House Rock.

Skirting it, we followed the trail onto Wickiup Plain, a broad, beige field of pumice and cinders broken only by sparse clumps of grass. Decades ago, Indian tribes gathered here each year for ceremonies and their brush wicki-ups covered the plain. We crossed it on a still, bright afternoon, and after so many weeks of forest paths I found it a welcome change to walk again in the open, to see the land forms slowly passing by. I watched LeConte Crater as it increased in size. A perfectly shaped cinder cone at the base of South Sister, it was swathed in a green velvet robe of grass. Contrasting with the serene beauty of the cone is the evidence of havoc the volcano caused a thousand years ago, a jumbled, craggy heap of lava named Rock Mesa.

We passed into the realm of Mesa Creek, a gentle meadow cut by several forks of a dancing creek, and followed one branch upstream to where it tumbled down an escarpment to nourish a garden of lupine.

A mist rolled in with the evening, wrapping our campsite in a delicate veil of coolness. As the fog wisped and eddied, the faint figure of a young black-tailed deer appeared no more than 30 feet from where we ate. It grazed awhile, gracefully leaped the creek, and vanished into the mist.

The beauty of Mesa Creek compelled us to stay another day. After breakfast we scrambled up the waterfall to its source where water seeped from among moss-covered stones. Cutting cross-country, we arrived at the foot of Rock Mesa, and I clambered up the lava flow to a vantage high above Mesa Creek. From here our distant tent was a spot of soft blue, and a pair of hikers striding through the valley looked like tiny animated figurines.

Clouds obscured the Three Sisters as we trudged past them next day, and our vision was channeled toward closer, smaller things: the water-polished skull of a deer in a small stream; glacial striations on the rocks; clusters of bright flowers along the trail; a bird drifting on the wind. Day's end brought us to a slender strand of water spilling over a 60-foot black cliff—Obsidian Falls, transformed by the last rays of sunlight into a sparkling diadem.

Dawn was one of the coldest in weeks. Still in my sleeping bag, I read the thermometer—it said 36°—and snuggled deeper into the warm cocoon. Somehow I talked Sam into getting up and brewing tea. With its warmth inside me, I gathered the nerve to jump out of the bag and throw on my clothes.

Within a mile we came upon a panorama of the major peaks ahead of us: Belknap Crater, Mount Washington, cloud-crowned Three Fingered Jack, Mount Jefferson, and—far in the distance—the hazy cone of Mount Hood. Behind us loomed North and Middle Sisters. Truly we were deep in the domain of the volcanic Cascades.

Mounds of black rock dwarfed us as we crunched and slipped our way to Oppie Dildock Pass, the trail's crest on a gigantic lava flow that originated from Collier Cone north of the Sisters. Here and there a solitary tree or bunch of grass formed a tiny oasis in the charcoal monochrome.

Lava shards kept working their way into my boots, and I had to stop often to shake them out. In the midst of this rugged, gray-black landscape, a yellow butterfly lighted on my hand. For several minutes it rode along, exploring the length of my arm before it flew off.

Near McKenzie Pass, amid a 65-square-mile wonderland of lava, the Pacific Crest Trail merges for a mile with McKenzie Highway. At the pass, Dee Wright Observatory, a small, turreted building constructed of volcanic rock, tops a knoll, and each of its many windows offers a view of a different mountain, from Shasta to Hood. Dee Wright was a packer for the Forest Service who helped build trail through the Sisters area and served as foreman of the crew that built the observatory. When he died in 1934, his ashes were scattered from an airplane to mingle with the volcanic ashes of this land he loved.

The remains of another man of pioneer stock rest in the lava near McKenzie Pass. In 1862, John Templeton Craig was hired to help build a road across the Cascades to link eastern and western Oregon. For 11 years he labored, sometimes alone, and finally in 1873 wagons rolled across the pass. In 1877, Craig was given the job of carrying mail over his road. At Christmastime he started on his first trip; a blizzard trapped him in a small cabin near the summit, and his body was found weeks later.

From McKenzie Pass, Sam and I hitchhiked down to the town of Sisters to pick up mail. Heat waves made the Three Sisters shimmer as we talked to 56-year-old postmaster Jess Edgington, a rawboned man who years ago worked as a packer in the Cascades. I asked him how the Three Sisters got their name. "Nobody knows for sure," he said, "but there's a story that in the 1840's a group of Methodists founding a mission over in Salem named the peaks Faith, Hope, and Charity. Sometime over the years the name was changed to the Three Sisters."

J. H. Belknap, an Oregon settler apparently less pious than the Methodists, named Belknap Crater for himself. A rounded, sloping hummock of lava, it has served as a practice ground for Apollo astronauts destined for the moon.

Traversing the Mount Washington Wilderness, we dipped to Santiam Pass and entered the Mount Jefferson Wilderness, surrounding the rocky bulk of its 10,497-foot namesake peak. On March 30, 1806 — on the homeward leg of their journey — Captains Meriwether Lewis and William Clark sighted this mountain from near the junction of the Willamette and Columbia Rivers. They named it for President Jefferson, who had selected them to explore the vast tract of land he had just acquired from France — land that stretched from the Mississippi River to the Pacific Ocean.

On our first night in the Mount Jefferson Wilderness we camped by a small pond dappled with water-lily pads. Fallen trees stretched into the water, colored a rich purplish brown by decaying vegetation. It was so quiet that the slightest sound caught my attention: the whir of a dragonfly's wings, the soft splash of a diving frog, the whispering of wind in the trees. That same breeze stirred the water and created the illusion that the lily pads were in motion, an armada of green rafts cruising the pond's surface.

Mount Jefferson drew nearer as we passed a series of sparkling lakes: Koko, with a convenient boulder for diving; Wasco, a delicate green sheet as seen from the trail atop a 300-foot bluff; Rockpile, where one morning Steve Van Sickle, a kindhearted packer, offered us leftover broiled steaks. "I always try to give extra steaks or eggs to backpackers," he explained, "because I know how much they appreciate it." We thanked him, packed the meat away, and set off as casually as we could. But around the first bend in the trail we ripped out our prize and had our earliest lunch yet: 9 a.m.!

Through the trail grapevine we learned about a new path that followed a higher elevation around Mount Jefferson and was fairly uncrowded. West of Cathedral Rocks, a serrated ridge reminiscent of the vaults and buttresses of a Gothic church, we cut cross-country until we stumbled onto the new section, then followed it high above Hunt's Cove to a group of small lakes. Snow-

"Barlow and his party inched their way across the Cascades."

flecked Jefferson rose above them, surrounded by lush meadows, groves of conifers, and outcrops of rock.

In this idyllic spot we stayed for two days, swimming, resting, talking with other hikers. One morning I lay on my back on the hillside and watched an extravaganza of clouds forming and dissipating. A west wind pushed its moisture up the slope of Jefferson; at a certain altitude, wisps of clouds started to coalesce. Growing puffier as they cartwheeled to the summit, they formed and reformed into a thousand shapes — faces, animals, abstract designs. Then, moving down the east side, they grew gradually smaller and finally trailed off into nothingness.

A deep call awakened me from a nap in time to see a large, slender bird with a six-foot wingspan — a sandhill crane, I think — swoop down to roost on a dead tree. The stately gray figure stood in sharp outline against the sky; then, gracefully, it took wing, circled the lake twice to gain altitude, and flew off.

During those quiet, reflective days near Mount Jefferson, I understood more clearly than ever John Muir's response to wilderness. "Nature's peace," he once wrote, "will flow into you as sunshine flows into trees."

But nature's peace was shattered one morning when a couple of dozen boys swarmed through the lake basin and began setting up camp — arguing over tent sites, complaining about blisters, chopping at downed trees, splashing in the lakes. Harried adults scurried about, making valiant but futile efforts at organization. Amused at the chaos, and glad we weren't part of it, we hurried off. The trail led us around the west flank of Jefferson and across several glacier-fed torrents to the meadows and lakes of Jefferson Park.

A thousand feet higher, as we hiked Park Ridge, we glimpsed Mount Hood for the first time in a week. On distant ridges we saw many large, bare tracts of land — the result of clear-cut timber harvesting. As we had progressed

into the Northwest, Sam and I had seen with increasing frequency these scars on the landscape where every bit of timber had been felled over a specified area. As we slid down the snowfields that abut Park Ridge and hiked out of the Mount Jefferson Wilderness, I decided to learn more about clear-cutting.

Considerably later, on a cold, overcast day in winter, I followed up on my intention. Emil Sabol, head of timber valuation for the U. S. Forest Service in Oregon and Washington, explained the process as we drove from his Portland office to a logging site on the northeast side of Mount Hood.

"Private industry has been clear-cutting since before the turn of the century," said this solid, muscular native of Michigan who has put in more than 25 years of field work with the Forest Service. "But it wasn't until after World War II, when the public began to make great demands for timber products, that we started it in the national forests.

"Clear-cutting is based on the attitude that a forest is a vast storehouse of wood that needs to be harvested, just like farm crops. We're lucky that wood is a renewable resource and a forest can be managed to reproduce itself, usually in about 80 to 150 years. And clear-cutting is a good, economical way of managing and harvesting timber. Even now, I'd say that only 50 percent of the harvesting we do is by the clear-cut method; the rest is by selective cutting—trimming out certain trees in a stand and leaving the rest to grow."

Wet snow began to splatter the windshield as we turned onto a side road. Sam asked about the Forest Service's relationship with environmentalists.

"We work with environmental groups as we plan our harvest areas, and we actively seek their recommendations. Before undertaking a cut, we also make an environmental analysis that tries to find out the impact on soil, water, wildlife. All this information is made public.

"Sure, there's an ugly-duckling stage to clear-cutting, but we're trying to minimize its impact. A new program that we call 'visual management' will make clear-cuts blend in better with the countryside. There's no doubt about it, those square postage-stamp cuts are eyesores. This new program will try to landscape the cuts to look like natural meadows.

"Another thing we're doing to help protect the land is called 'skyline yarding.' Instead of building logging roads, or skidding the logs across the earth and scarring the soil, we suspend them from overhead cables and let them ride downhill to the trucks. Helicopter logging is another new technique."

As he spoke, a large helicopter approached with three logs dangling at the end of a 150-foot cable. Whipping the trees like a summer thunderstorm, it hovered over a clearing, lowered the logs to within two feet of the ground, released them, and flew off. The concussion of the logs' impact shook me. As they bounced to rest, two men hurried out and released the cables binding them together. A front-end loader grabbed them in its jaws to stack them. The helicopter promptly swept into view again with another load. I looked at my watch; the circuit had taken exactly 2½ minutes.

"This is one of the most unusual kinds of flying," Jim Weatherill told me during his short lunch break. A former Army aviator who flew helicopters in Viet Nam, the mustachioed Weatherill is now a command pilot for Columbia

Helicopters, Inc. Black tousled hair curled from under a crumpled felt hat as he ate from a can of tuna. "Instead of watching the horizon, you fly the hook — looking straight down the cable at the logs. It takes a lot of precision and a lot of concentration."

Later that afternoon, another helicopter landed me near the clear-cutting site. Ashen clouds loomed above, and a light snow melted on my hard hat and dripped down my neck. I watched as Weatherill's helicopter streaked up the valley toward me; its wash churned the cold air and blew off my hard hat. Through this maelstrom Jim lowered the hook directly into the hands of a man waiting to attach the logs. Smoothly the pilot raised the craft; the logs broke free of clinging branches and in moments were whisked down the valley.

Jim Crider, a logger standing beside me, shook his head and smiled. "I been logging for 25 years, from New Mexico to Alaska, but this is something else. I still haven't gotten used to it."

As we returned to Portland I reflected on the deep differences of opinion with respect to clear-cutting. Most veterans of the timber industry tend to look on trees in economic terms — as a harvestable crop — and many advocate clear-cutting not only as an efficient way to harvest but also as an effective means of forest regeneration. Others argue for selective cutting; they and the environmentalists, who stress the beauty and ecological importance of old-growth stands of timber, are concerned about the effects of clear-cutting in terms of erosion, stream pollution, and the whole fragile forest ecosystem. Even those who favor clear-cutting agree that there are areas where it should not be practiced, because of esthetic considerations or because the climatic conditions make regeneration of trees difficult.

A friend once showed me something that forester Aldo Leopold wrote in the 1920's: "We abuse land because we regard it as a commodity belonging to us. When we see land as a community to which we belong, we may begin to use it with love and respect."

We started our last hike in Oregon at Timberline Lodge, a massive resort hotel located 6,000 feet high on the flank of Mount Hood and just a few hundred yards from the Pacific Crest Trail. The building itself is a fascinating, one-of-a-kind structure built and decorated during the Great Depression by laborers, craftsmen, and artists employed by the Works Progress Administration. A popular ski facility in winter, it was thronged with summer vacationers when we passed through the hexagonal central hall to the dining room.

For more than a century and a half, people have been crossing this part of Oregon on their way to and from the coastal valleys. In the early 1800's a stream of settlers pointed wagons west on the Oregon Trail. Starting at Independence, Missouri, they crossed 2,000 miles of prairies, hills, and rugged mountains, but when they reached the towering Cascades their path was blocked. The only gateway to the fertile lands lying between the mountains and the Pacific Ocean was the Columbia River, and the rough-and-tumble raft trip down this raging waterway was a dangerous proposition.

In the fall of 1845 a resolute man named Samuel Barlow, rebelling at the expense and risk of the boat trip, boldly declared, "God never made a mountain but what He provided a place for man to go over or around it."

With a small company, Barlow set out to find an overland route south of Mount Hood. By hacking their way through the wilderness, whipping the oxen uphill, and lowering the wagons downhill by ropes, Barlow and his party inched their way across the Cascades. When winter overtook them, they left the vehicles and continued to Oregon City on foot and horseback. The next spring Barlow and others returned and improved the route, and by late summer of 1846 settlers were traversing Barlow's road in a week's time at a toll of five dollars a wagon and a dime a head for livestock. In a chivalrous gesture, he permitted "widow women" to pass free of charge.

North of Timberline Lodge the Pacific Crest Trail ducks in and out of several steep-walled canyons, some dry and dusty, others pulsing with icy runoff from Hood's glaciers. In Zigzag Canyon a muffled roar drew us upstream to a 75-foot waterfall, where we lingered in the cool spray.

Paradise Park, a rolling meadow dominated by Mount Hood, was congested with backpackers. We camped well away from the crowds beside a huge, round, grayish white boulder that we christened Skull Rock. At dusk a rusty alpenglow outlined Mount Hood; to the south, Mount Jefferson turned a delicate rose, and long wisps of clouds hung in the sky above it like windblown tresses. At dawn we found a different display of color in an alpine garden fed by a spring: brilliant red Indian paintbrush, lavender lupine, and countless small flowers of yellow and white.

From a cushion of mountain heather atop Indian Mountain, one of the last high ridges before the Columbia River, I looked down on a valley cut by a stream that drops 3,000 feet in ten miles. Southbound hikers had praised the beauty of that route down Eagle Creek, and we decided to take a short detour from the main trail.

Eagle Creek Trail parallels the creek, sometimes carved into the canyon wall hundreds of feet above the stream bed, occasionally following right beside its dozens of cascades and quiet pools. At Tunnel Falls the trail, chiseled from solid rock halfway up a cliff, cuts in *behind* the falls. From that little cavern I peered out through a roaring sheet of plunging, crystal-clear water.

We raced approaching dusk down the last few miles of Eagle Creek and into the broad gorge of the Columbia. As we paused near the riverside highway at the base of the cliffs, a huge copper moon rose out of the water. Framed by the walls of the gorge, it shed a diffused light that wrought subtle changes and obscured the marks of man—the dams, the bridges, the railroads, the power lines, the road cuts. Like Lewis and Clark long before me, I beheld a land of serene beauty, a land "grateful to the eye."

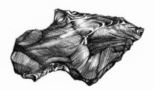

Beyond a veil of hemlock boughs, a slender waterfall plunges into Eagle Creek near the Columbia River gorge. Of such falls John Muir wrote, "...how delightful the water music...the clashing, ringing spray."

ABOVE: OBSIDIAN POINT FOUND BY THE AUTHOR

*"I glanced into a
darkening meadow
and was startled
to see a
prehistoric monster
lurking there..."*

Gnarled and weathered, a fallen tree

becomes a dragon-like apparition at the forest's edge near Long Lake.

Sawdust and wood chips fly as a logger with a chain saw cuts a felled hemlock into specified lengths in Mount Hood National Forest. Logging in such scenic areas often brings environmentalists and businessmen into bitter conflict; the scars — access roads through the forest, gouges made by dragged logs — can remain for years. At left, a new tool minimizes such damage: A helicopter hoists ponderosa pine and Douglas fir to a truck-loading site. A fire to warm workers burns in the foreground.

Clouds race their shadows across Crater Lake, whose waters reach 1,932 feet deep within

a huge collapsed volcano. A miniature crater tops Wizard Island, itself a volcanic cone.

Campfire brightens a foggy evening in a meadow of the Three Sisters Wilderness. A timid black-tailed deer pauses warily nearby, ghostly in the mist. Will and Sam cooked on a lightweight alcohol stove, rarely building a fire except in extremely cold weather or when they needed to dry out. At this peaceful spot near Mesa Creek, they camped for an extra day, exploring upstream to the creek's rockbound source.

*"A mist rolled in with the evening,
wrapping our campsite
in a delicate veil of coolness."*

*"I'm a teacher, a friend,
and the final arbiter on questions of safety,
but the kids learn a lot on their own."*

Sharing her love of the outdoors with the
oncoming generation, Susan Kreitzberg
tours the Mount Hood area in summer as a
guide and counselor for groups of teen-agers.
Here she conducts a class in knot-tying.
During their week-long treks, sponsored
by the American Wilderness Foundation, the
youngsters study nature and practice survival
skills. Deep cream-yellow bear grass and bright
splashes of wild flowers — lavender lupine,
red Indian paintbrush, white bistort,
yellow groundsel — carpet their classroom.

Dawn breaks beneath the clouds as climbers make their way up a snow-

crusted ridge of Mount Hood, at 11,235 feet the highest peak in Oregon.

*"Plunge stepping" cautiously through deep snow, Geographic picture editor
Dave Bridge descends Mount Hood, negotiating a much steeper slope than the
camera angle suggests. Eighteen climbers have lost their lives at this
treacherous spot near the summit. At right, his climbing partners flank
Dave: Sam on his right, Barry Bishop, who climbed Mount Everest in 1963,
on his left. Sam unfurls the banner of the Toad Hall Explorers Club, an
organization he co-founded — "It had two members" — while in college.*

MISTY ROCKS, RIVERS OF ICE

7

"THE SASQUATCH? An enormous creature, maybe nine feet tall and a thousand pounds. He has dark hair all over, like a bear, but always walks upright like a man. People have claimed to see sasquatches from northern California up into Alaska. Even a couple of my friends, men whose word I respect, have reported spotting a sasquatch or finding its tracks."

Ken Walkington, a member of the headquarters staff of Gifford Pinchot National Forest in southern Washington, was telling Sam and me about the legendary apeman of North America. Called sasquatch by the Indians of British Columbia, and bigfoot, abominable snowman, American yeti, or omah by various other people, the creature has contributed to the lore of the Pacific Northwest for more than a hundred years. During that time some 750 sightings have been recorded, but little supporting evidence exists.

"There are a few plaster casts and photographs of large footprints," Ken said, "and there's one short, jerky movie sequence of something large and hairy walking through a meadow. But it's hard to judge any of these."

When Sam asked Ken if he believed the sasquatch stories, he smiled and shrugged. "I'm not ready to say. To pass judgment I'd need some personal proof. You two may find something before I do—southern Washington is the heart of sasquatch country, and you'll be hiking right through it."

If this was the right place, it apparently was not the right time, and we saw nothing to contribute to the sasquatch legend as we made our way northward. But we did find tangible reminders of other Northwest lore. Thirty trail miles north of the Columbia we entered Indian Heaven, a rolling, meadowed expanse of huckleberry patches and tiny lakes stretching almost to Mount Adams. For centuries the Yakima Indians and other tribes gathered here in the autumn to harvest the wild berries and to hold contests and ceremonials. At Indian Racetrack only a rutted path overgrown with windblown grass evokes the echo of a time when horses and riders thundered by in hard-fought

At the Pacific Crest Trail's highest point in Washington—7,620 feet, on the north shoulder of Old Snowy Mountain—Will and Linda Gray stop to rest while orienting a map of the Goat Rocks Wilderness surrounding them.

races for status and prizes. The excitement and pageantry are gone, but one tradition of Indian Heaven persists. In autumn, when dark blue huckleberries hang heavy on the bushes, Yakima Indians still congregate here from their reservation east of the trail. They put up tepees and harvest berries from 800 acres of national forest land reserved by treaty solely for their use. According to Yakima belief the huckleberry, along with venison and salmon, is a sacred food that signifies nature's bounty.

As we crossed Indian Heaven, soaring Mount Adams—at 12,307 feet the third highest peak in the Cascades, after Rainier and Shasta—loomed ahead of us. Before entering the Mount Adams Wilderness, however, I left the trail and drove to Seattle to meet my wife, Linda, who was joining Sam and me for the two weeks of her vacation. Barely five feet and a hundred pounds, Linda nevertheless carried her 35-pound pack with assurance and complained of few of the first-day aches and blisters common to most backpackers.

Along the west side of Mount Adams the Pacific Crest Trail holds to an almost-level contour just above timberline. But to reach that elevation we had to climb a long, forested ridge; when we finally broke into the open, we stopped for the day. At dusk Linda and I clambered up a rock outcrop to a spectacular view dominated in each direction by a major peak. To the east were the blue-gray rocky walls of Mount Adams; to the north was misty Mount Rainier; to the west, like a pyramid of snow, stood Mount St. Helens; and to the south, across the Columbia, rose the white cap of Mount Hood.

Morning brought a drizzling rain that by noon had changed to a dreary gray mist. In our first mile we came upon a remarkable sight—a waterfall of moss. Extending down the steep hillside was a curtain of soft green that completely screened the small spring that nurtured it.

A few steps farther on we met Richard and Laura Kinne, a California couple in their mid-20's who had been hiking south from the Canadian border for 48 days. A bulky bundle covered with yellow plastic rode at the back of Richard's pack. When I asked about it, Laura seemed a little embarrassed, but Richard proudly explained, "Laura's a schoolteacher by profession but an artist at heart. Those are the paintings she's made on this trip."

Encouraged by Linda and Sam, Laura unwrapped her work. To our delight she slowly leafed through the paintings: trail scenes and details of nature, captured with delicate watercolors in a graceful, impressionistic style.

She came to the last one. "I just painted it this morning. It's a waterfall on Killen Creek, a couple of miles north of here." With the painting fresh in our minds, we continued to Killen Creek. Lovely as the actual scene was, we agreed that Laura had done it justice.

The creek flows over a tilted escarpment, creating a 40-foot cascade of white water on black rock. At the bottom the churning water soon quiets, and winds across a meadow like a gentle millstream. In this setting we hurriedly set up our tent, for rain began to fall again and the temperature to plummet. We raised our nylon tarp as a portico and beneath it ate our supper while the rain slowly turned to sleet.

As the particles of ice ticked on the taut nylon above us, we watched the sleet thicken and then become a dense, silent snowfall—the first August snowstorm for any of us. The ground rapidly turned white. Knocking the first accumulation from the roof, Sam, Linda, and I crowded into our two-man tent and quickly fell asleep.

The new day invaded our shelter and drew us outside, where a pure white blanket an inch deep masked everything. Above the snow-decked waterfall rose venerable Mount Adams, its glaciers clean and bright with fresh snow. Suddenly I felt a special kinship with that great prominence. During my trip I had discovered that mountains seemed to take on individual personalities as I spent time near them; and Adams, I thought, projected the friendliest personality yet.

The August snowstorm was followed by a warm rain that started to wash away the white cover. We left the Mount Adams Wilderness and crossed several miles of open brushland to reach Midway Guard Station, where supplies awaited us. The small frame house nestles next to Midway Creek at the intersection of two dirt roads, only a few dozen yards from the trail.

Linda's knock at the front door brought one of the two summer rangers, a tall, dark young woman with piercing brown eyes. She welcomed us warmly, identified herself as Joan Bird, and started stoking up the cast-iron stove as we stripped off our rain gear. Tousle-haired Sandy Spurling, the other ranger, promptly brought us steaming mugs of tea and huckleberry tarts that she and Joan had baked.

They invited us to spend the night in the two-room cabin, and we decided to pool our resources for supper. Huckleberry muffins and the fresh salad greens they kept chilled in Midway Creek deliciously complemented our freeze-dried meat. More tarts finished off the meal.

Rain drummed on the roof as we ate, and continued as we stretched out around the stove. The flames and glowing coals sent a dancing pattern of light

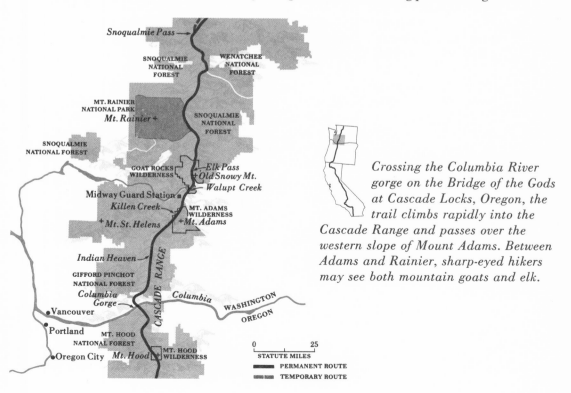

Crossing the Columbia River gorge on the Bridge of the Gods at Cascade Locks, Oregon, the trail climbs rapidly into the Cascade Range and passes over the western slope of Mount Adams. Between Adams and Rainier, sharp-eyed hikers may see both mountain goats and elk.

through the grate to play across the room. We learned that Sandy worked as the recreation guard and Joan was responsible for the fire patrol. "Our duties aren't that formalized, though, and we help each other," Joan said. Sandy explained that a lot of their time was spent answering questions and helping hikers, campers, and berry-pickers. "But we did have some excitement a couple of weeks ago — we helped fight a series of fires caused by lightning. Joan and I are the first women in our district ever to work on the fire line."

Under a bright sun the next morning we ate breakfast outdoors; then, after dividing and packing our new stock of food, we headed north toward the Goat Rocks Wilderness. Just inside the wilderness boundary a high, bald hill gave us a panorama of the Goat Rocks, a long, jagged ridge of crumbly volcanic rock streaked by snow and glaciers.

As we walked down into Coleman Weedpatch, a level section of meadows and pines, I noticed the fresh tracks of a large animal in the loose dust of the trail. Five inches long and three wide, they bore an unsettling resemblance to the tracks of a small bear, and I began to envision a cub moving merrily down the trail while an irritable mother bear followed in the grass nearby. My apprehension increased abruptly when, at the top of a short, steep hill, we heard a rustling in the brush to our left.

Then I laughed. Walking toward us, his huge tail sweeping the air, was one of the largest dogs I have ever seen. His shoulders reached to the middle of my thigh. He nuzzled me, licked my hand, and lolled his head with pleasure as Linda and I ran our hands through his thick, woolly white hair. A young man walked up to us; his curly hair and thick beard seemed to match the texture of the dog's coat. "I'm sorry Benedictus startled you," he said. "One couple who saw him from a distance swore that he was a polar bear."

Introducing himself as Jim Hesser, a predivinity student from Pennsylvania, he told us that Benedictus — Ben for short — was a Great Pyrenees, a European sheepherding breed. Amazed at Ben's size, Linda asked if he was full-grown. "Oh, no," Jim laughed, "he's still a pup — only nine months old. He weighs about 100 pounds now, and may get to be twice that before he stops." Linda and I both thought of Trevor, our little Shetland sheepdog; we considered him a pretty solid animal at 25 pounds.

Jim accepted our invitation to hike with us for a few days. He strapped on Ben's saddlebags, climbed into his own pack, and stuck an unlit pipe in his mouth. "Ben carries his own food and dishes, as well as our tent and some of my food — it makes it easier for me."

Perhaps because of his breed's long heritage of herding, Ben walked last in line and kept watch over us. When someone stopped or wandered off, Ben circled around and urged the hiker back toward the trail. I had never hiked with a more attentive companion.

As we continued through Coleman Weedpatch, Linda spotted two black-tailed deer grazing in a meadow overflowing with bluebells and the white blossoms of pearly everlasting. Then we angled up a long ridge to Walupt Creek, a mere trickle of water, and camped in its meadow. At supper we celebrated Linda's 25th birthday. I was ready to toast her with a draught of creek water when Sam surprised us; digging into the deep recesses of his pack, he produced a water container filled with wine. "I got this when I first learned about Linda's birthday," he announced with a flourish as he poured us each a cupful. Several days in a plastic container bouncing in Sam's hot pack had not improved the bouquet of the wine, but we were the least critical of connoisseurs; we found it exquisite. Even Ben enjoyed a small ration.

As we made our way along the west wall of the Goat Rocks the next two days, Linda and I kept scanning the heights for a glimpse of one of the shaggy white mountain goats that account for the area's name. The low-hanging clouds didn't help visibility, and our hopes went unfulfilled.

After a damp, windy night on a knoll 300 feet above Snowgrass Flat, Jim and Ben left us to return to their car at Midway Guard Station. Sam, Linda, and I roused ourselves for the 1,400-foot climb to the crest of the Goat Rocks. The mist shrouding the ridge inspired Sam to rename it Ghost Rocks.

Near the top of Old Snowy Mountain we attained the Pacific Crest Trail's highest point in Washington—7,620 feet. Ahead of us a yard-wide trail snaked off into the swirling, windblown mist; on either side the rocks dropped off precipitously to foggy nothingness. From the maps I knew that active glaciers, Packwood to the west and McCall to the east, rumbled hundreds of feet below, yet we seemed suspended in a realm that extended less than 50 feet in any direction.

For two miles the trail threaded the crest of this sharp ridge. The wind, gusting to 40 miles an hour, pushed at us viciously. At 180 pounds I felt firmly anchored, but I worried about Linda, who often staggered in a heavy blast.

As we approached Elk Pass an amazing change occurred—for a moment. The wind stopped, the mist cleared, the sun appeared. A grassy, gently sloping valley opened before us, and on the horizon Packwood Lake shimmered with a golden reflection of the sun. Then the clouds closed in, and we hiked on to the pass with everything around us again obscured.

At Elk Pass the trail drops off the crest and descends steeply to a field of gravel cut by a glacial stream. Exhausted yet exhilarated by our unusual day, we crawled into the tent to escape the wind. In the middle of the night I awoke to the sound of silence. The raging wind had abated, but it left us a sagging tent; so I braved the cold to reset the poles and retie the ropes, and was rewarded with a sky ablaze with stars—the first in several nights.

Morning brought another revelation. Only 30 miles away, rising from a throne of low clouds, shone the regal presence of Mount Rainier, soaring to 14,410 feet. With our next major objective in sight, we packed up quickly and hiked out of the Goat Rocks to see Linda aboard a plane for home.

Sam and I returned to Rainier the same week with high hopes of climbing the majestic peak. But the warmth of late summer had brought crumbling ice and unstable rock conditions, and we were advised not to attempt the climb. So—for the time being—we shelved our plans.

As it turned out, it was almost ten months before we came back to Mount Rainier National Park. By mid-July the threat of late spring storms was past, but deep, firm snow still covered the mountain's wide shoulders, promising the year's best and safest climbing conditions. For this part of our adventure Sam and I separated temporarily. I arranged to climb with Ben Englebright, a ranger from Glacier Peak Wilderness whom I had met the summer before; Sam joined two National Geographic colleagues, Barry C. Bishop, who in 1963 had climbed Mount Everest, and David R. Bridge, the picture editor of this book, to follow a different route. Before their climb the three headed for Mount Hood to attend a mountaineering school.

Accompanying Ben, Doug Gosling, and me were Dave Clemens, a forester making his second ascent of Mount Rainier; Sue Clemens, his wife; and Tim Place, a slight, bewhiskered young climber whose goals include scaling all of the 19 peaks in Washington that rise above 9,000 feet.

After packing for our three-day journey, we moved out from mile-high Paradise Ranger Station onto the white mantle of Rainier and began the five-hour march to Camp Muir. For Doug and me this was an important training session; our previous mountain climbing had not required specialized ice and snow techniques. Ben, who teaches mountaineering and wilderness survival at Skagit Valley College in Mount Vernon, Washington, explained and demonstrated — and Doug and I practiced — such fundamentals as how to use the foot spikes called crampons on ice; how to arrest a fall properly with an ice ax; how to travel safely on a rope team.

A climber of long experience, Ben is also a patient instructor and an ever-pleasant companion. His iron-gray hair and furrowed face contrast with a boyish smile and a sparkle in his ice-blue eyes. At 61 he blends the wisdom of age with the vigor of youth, and combines a love of the land with an understanding and warm regard for people.

In early afternoon we crested a bare rock ridge exactly 10,000 feet high and found Camp Muir, a collection of flat-roofed stone structures. Two of the buildings, a bunkhouse and a kitchen, belong to Rainier Mountaineering, Inc., a commercial guide service. Mountaineers not on a guided climb sleep under the stars, or in a public shelter that has space for 25.

We loafed at Camp Muir the rest of the afternoon; the extended rest period was an essential part of our acclimatization for the altitude ahead. Our plan called for rising at one o'clock in the morning to begin the ascent. "There's less chance then of an avalanche, or of a snowbridge collapsing into a crevasse," Tim explained.

After eating supper and melting snow for drinking water for the next day, I crawled into my sleeping bag, which I had positioned on a rock shelf that provided a view of the mountain. Evening transformed Rainier into a dark, brooding giant. Above it the sky became a vast starscape, its countless twinkling points of light the brightest of the trip.

The night had only begun, it seemed, when Ben shook me awake. After a quick breakfast, we were ready to start. I strapped on my crampons, hooked the rope linking Ben, Tim, and me into the harness around my chest and waist, and grasped ice ax and flashlight in mittened hands. A moment later our rope team stepped onto half-mile-wide Cowlitz Glacier, our first obstacle. Almost immediately Ben, in the lead, dipped out of sight. I quickly found out why. A great wrinkle in the ice took me almost straight down 30 feet, then back up the other side. As my crampons bit into the ice and the ax helped provide balance, my confidence in both my equipment and myself suddenly increased.

Halfway across Cowlitz I switched off my flashlight and walked by the faint illumination of the moon. After I took a giant step over my first crevasse—all of three inches wide—we crossed an area littered with stony debris from a steep, narrow ridge called Cathedral Rocks at the glacier's edge.

Stumbling up a steep slope of crumbly talus, we reached the crest of the ridge leading to the top of Cathedral Rocks just as sunrise began to tint the undersides of the gray clouds a soft pink. Soon the sun broke over the horizon and cast an orange glow on the ice of Mount Rainier.

We moved up the sloping bulk of Ingraham Glacier until we were momentarily stopped by a gigantic ice fall, a jumble of huge blocks each as large as a five-story building and rent by gaping crevasses. Edging past this monumental mass of ice, we began to labor up the outcrop of rock and snow called Disappointment Cleaver. The steepest pitch of the whole climb took us to its top, a vertical rise of 1,500 feet in less than half a mile.

After a short rest, we began to zigzag toward the summit, carefully skirting ice falls and choosing the safest places to cross the many crevasses. At the first one we had to jump—a gash about three feet wide—I watched Tim hop lightly across and decided that, since I was several inches taller, I would have even less trouble. When I got to the edge, however, I looked down at least a hundred feet into the blue-green interior of the glacier, and suddenly I was

"I knitted together
my courage
and leaped..."

hypnotized. Finally I knitted together my courage, recovered command of my legs, and leaped; I easily cleared the crevasse, but I had jumped with such determination that I fell forward into a snowbank on the other side.

On wider crevasses we secured the rope around a partially buried ice ax; if the person jumping should slip, his fall would be arrested at once.

A dormant volcano, Mount Rainier is topped by a cup-shaped crater 400 yards in diameter. We breached the crater rim at a rocky low spot; directly across from us a mound of snow 50 feet above our level identified Columbia Crest, the mountain's pinnacle.

To escape the brunt of the cold wind that constantly sweeps the rim, we dropped into the snow-filled crater, where we found a cluster of snow shelters built by earlier climbers. Some were aboveground windbreaks made of thick blocks of snow; others were elaborate subterranean igloos.

In midafternoon, leaving our packs behind, we walked across the crater and began to climb. Finally I reached a hump of snow from which everything around me sloped downhill, and I knew I was standing on the crown of Mount Rainier. The exhilaration that has always raced through me at the top of a great mountain overtook me again. A vast panorama surrounded me, from central Oregon to British Columbia, from eastern Washington to the Pacific Ocean. I recognized a whole gallery of familiar peaks—Jefferson, Hood, Adams, St. Helens, the Goat Rocks—but I was standing on what I and many others consider the most majestic mountain along the entire Pacific Crest Trail.

Near a large boulder slightly below the summit, we signed our names in a climbers' register. A few feet away I noticed evidence of Rainier's latent volcanism: A jet of steam rushed from a tiny vent in the ground.

At various places throughout the crater, steam has melted the snow and ice to form a labyrinth of passageways and chambers below the surface. At the crater wall I squeezed between ice and rock and found myself in part of this network. In 1870, the first men to climb Rainier were overtaken by darkness at the top but survived by passing the night in such a steam cave.

Carrying a small flashlight, I slid down a steep rock pile under a low ceiling of ice dimpled by uneven melting. Suddenly the narrow corridor opened up, and I peered into a large cavern at least a hundred feet wide and twenty high. My light barely penetrated the blackness of that misty crypt. An involuntary shiver went up my spine, and I scrambled quickly back to daylight.

That night, as I crawled into bed in one of the igloos, my weariness was offset by a sense of deep satisfaction. Now I knew mighty Rainier firsthand, its glaciers and rocks, its wind and cold, even some of its inner secrets. Snugly sheltered below the surface of the crater's ice pack, I drifted into sleep.

Californian Richard Kinne explains a detail in his wife Laura's watercolor of Killen Creek, near Mount Adams. Laura painted more than 30 scenes along the trail in Washington as the couple hiked south from Canada.

ABOVE: SNOW CRYSTALS

Rearing above the surrounding clouds, 12,307-foot Mount Adams
looms blue and white in the summer sun. Like Mount Hood and
other major peaks in the Cascade Range, Adams formed more than
half a million years ago from volcanic upheaval. Farther north, Will
and Linda concentrate on their footing as they cross the Goat Rocks
Wilderness, a bleak, windswept land of crumbling volcanic debris.

*"There rose venerable
Mount Adams,
its glaciers clean and
bright with fresh snow."*

Mist swirls around a treeless ridge of the Goat Rocks, here the crest line of the Cascades.

Chilled by the strong wind, Will pulls on a heavy shirt.

Afternoon sun burnishing her hair, Joan Bird rests on a bridge over Midway Creek. Joan, assigned fire patrol duty, and recreation guard Sandy Spurling (below) shared a cabin at Midway Guard Station between Mount Adams and the Goat Rocks. Among the first women hired by the Forest Service as summer rangers, Joan and Sandy spent much of their time helping hikers and campers but also served on the fire line. In a high meadow beside Walupt Creek, Benedictus, a half-grown Great Pyrenees (above), tussles gently with his owner, predivinity student Jim Hesser.

His aircraft safely hangared, Jim Beech, operator of Rain Air Scenic Flights in Ashford, Washington, heads across the meadow (opposite) that borders his runway. For 21 years Beech has navigated over Mount Rainier, perfecting his knowledge of wind currents and terrain while flying search and rescue missions as well as sightseeing tours. At right, he confirms the location of a hiker far below.

*Treacherous icefall on the south side
of Mount Rainier gives expert climber
Lute Jerstad a chance to practice
some of the skills that helped him reach
the top of Mount Everest in 1963.
Although towering 14,410 feet above
sea level, Rainier offers routes for
novice as well as experienced mountaineers. Inside its volcanic crater,
Will (below) peers into a snow shelter
built by earlier climbers to protect
them from the biting winds.*

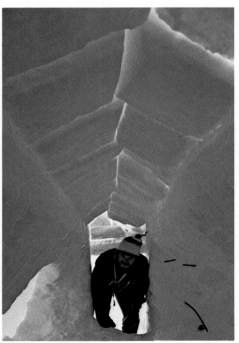

DOUG GOSLING (ABOVE)

CASCADE AUTUMN: NORTH TO THE BORDER

8

AMERICA'S ALPS, mountaineers reverently call the North Cascades: craggy peaks, serrated ridges, plunging valleys, and 750 glaciers in a vast and splendid jumble reaching from Snoqualmie Pass to the Canadian border. Despite the massive cones of Glacier Peak and Mount Baker, most of the northern range is geologically distinct from the volcanic Cascades farther south, and the North Cascades have had a complex history of folding, faulting, and erosion that geologists only now are gradually puzzling out.

This rugged wonderland, cut by 238 miles of the Pacific Crest Trail, stretched before us as we stood at Snoqualmie Pass. With us for our push to the border were Doug Gosling and willowy, brown-haired Ellen Smith, who, like Doug, had been a high school student of Sam's in Ohio.

Red Mountain was our first obstacle; the trail climbed 2,000 feet on switchbacks, then descended 3,000 feet to the Middle Fork of the Snoqualmie River. As we walked toward Dutch Miller Gap, we noticed a few tinges of fall; dwarf maples were starting to turn yellow, huckleberry bushes scarlet, and mountain ash trees orange. That evening the crisp air nipped at us, and we huddled close to the fire, rubbing mittened hands on chilly legs.

A light fog settled in as we neared the headwaters of the Middle Fork. Out of the mist walked a man wearing a khaki baseball cap and carrying a shovel. His name was Bob Norton, and as trail engineer for Snoqualmie National Forest he obviously preferred the field to his desk. "I try to walk as many miles as possible in Snoqualmie Forest every year, to find out for myself what shape the trail is in," he said. As he talked he kept working, clearing a clump of brush at the trail's edge, shoveling dirt to fill a muddy spot.

We learned that Bob had been on the staff here for 25 years. "In a couple of days you'll be walking the trail from Deception Pass to Deception Lakes. That was one of the first sections I ever worked, and it's still my favorite."

Dutch Miller Gap is a grassy plateau dotted with small pools and large

Harvesting fall's bounty, Will gathers berries beneath craggy Lichtenberg Mountain in central Washington. From here, the trail skirts volcanic hot springs and year-round snowfields as it winds northward to Canada.

boulders. Sam likened it to a spacious Japanese rock garden. Several hundred feet below the gap lies dagger-shaped Lake Ivanhoe. By the time we reached it, a cold wind was whipping up whitecaps and a light rain had begun to fall, and we quickly made camp on a small promontory.

That night I awoke with a start and felt a strange sensation in my hair, then heard a scurrying sound. As I turned on my flashlight, a pair of tiny brown mice dashed the length of my sleeping bag, swerved, and ran across Sam's. Then, to my amazement, they returned for another circuit. When they began their third pass, I sat up and chased them out the end of the tent. North Cascade mice, I decided, are anything but timid.

We left the rain clouds of Lake Ivanhoe next day and dropped 1,700 feet in elevation toward the slender mirror of Waptus Lake. On the way we found another harbinger of the change of seasons. Doug observed an industrious pika—a small, chubby relative of the rabbit with a high, squeaky voice—preparing for winter: "He looked all around, then ran over to a stand of lupine, bit off several stalks at ground level, and carried them in his mouth to his burrow. He left them there on the ground and went back for more." Since he doesn't hibernate, the pika must store a large supply of winter food, and may gather as much as a bushel.

Descending from Cathedral Rock to Hyas Lake, we were startled by a gunshot, followed by two more in rapid succession. A few minutes later we came upon a pair of hunters, one of whom gruffly reminded us that it was the first day of goat and deer season and that we'd better be careful. Appreciating his warning if not his manner, I quickly fished out my red bandana and tied it to the top of my pack—and left it there for the next two weeks.

Hunting is prohibited in national parks but not in national forests. As we moved down the steep grade toward the lake, we heard rifle reports every few minutes. A road penetrates almost to the lake, and we found 50 cars and dozens of hunters thronging the dusty parking lot. But we left most of the hunters behind as we climbed Deception Pass and followed a forest trail contoured for easy grades—Bob Norton's favorite section—to Deception Lakes, a pair of emerald pools studded with boulders.

Toiling slowly along the edge of Surprise Mountain next morning, I looked ahead 40 or 50 yards and realized that a mule deer was peering back at me. Apparently deciding that we posed no threat, he started up the trail like a fellow backpacker. We had followed him half a mile when we heard the bark of a rifle shot. We froze in place—though there was no indication that the shot was aimed in our direction—but the deer was too wise to wait. He leaped up an almost vertical embankment and disappeared into the underbrush.

We were approaching Lake Susan Jane when I saw two hikers, rucksacks on their backs, climbing toward us at a brisk pace. Soon we were pausing for a greeting and a brief conversation. "We're Franklin and Hildur Blocksom," said the man. "We're on our way to some huckleberry patches we know. Want to lay in a supply for canning."

Tall and lean, he had pale blue eyes that matched the morning sky. They brightened in amusement when he asked me to guess his age. I estimated 62, and he chuckled. "Wrong. I'm 76, and Hildur here is 75"—he grabbed her hand—"and we've pulled each other through some pretty tight knotholes.

"Three years ago we were floating down the Colorado River in the Grand Canyon on air mattresses with a rafting party, and Hildur got separated from the rest. But finally the red ribbon on her hat appeared around the bend—she was alone but safe—and, well, here we are."

The Blocksoms have led an adventurous life—even more so since he retired as a Government engineer working in Alaska. "We've traveled all over North America," said Hildur, whose warm smile softened the intense blue of her eyes. "We've gone all through Mexico, and taken a boat—just the two of us—down the Yukon River. We're going to do that again one of these years."

Franklin changed the subject. "Right now our main concern is our mine near Twisp, Washington. We still operate it, with the help of three miners. It was discovered back in the '90's and later abandoned; we staked part of it in 1939 and bought the rest in 1941. We expect to hit it rich soon."

Enchanted with this vibrant couple, Sam asked for their advice, expecting some comment on health and longevity. But without a moment's hesitation Franklin replied, "Watch your finances. Plan for your future. Then enjoy that future." Still hand in hand, he and Hildur resumed their climb.

High tension wires slicing across the trail heralded our approach to Stevens Pass, a popular winter ski resort, but in September only a gasoline station and cafe showed any signs of activity. We headed for Lake Valhalla six miles to the north, following Stevens Creek through a narrow valley decked with the reds and golds of autumn. As we walked, Doug, steeped in the lore of his Norse ancestors, told us stories of Valhalla, the heaven of Viking warriors. Time passed quickly, and the sun had gone down when we arrived at the lake. With the black outline of Lichtenberg Mountain rising above us, we watched the sunset color the lake in deepening shades of burgundy and mauve. After a while a full moon climbed from behind the mountain and threw a shaft of light across the lake.

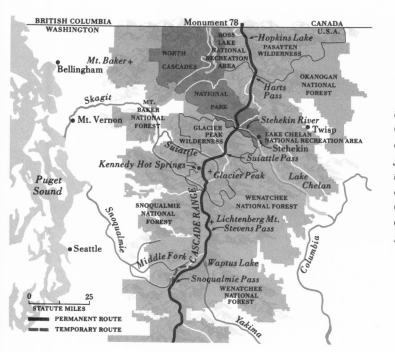

From Snoqualmie Pass to the Canadian border, the trail covers 238 rugged miles as it hugs the ridges of Washington's North Cascades. Here heavy snows close off most of the route until July. To enter Canada by way of the trail, hikers must make advance arrangements with the Canadian port of entry in Osoyoos or Huntington, British Columbia.

179

Just above Valhalla next morning we found a stand of laden huckleberry bushes, and picked the fat, ripe berries until we had filled a quart pot as well as our stomachs.

Evening caught us at the top of Grizzly Peak, a broad, exposed ridge of yellow grasses and a few stunted pines. Gusting and moaning, a wind lashed the east side of the ridge and raced across its meadowed crown. By luck we stumbled on a copse of trees with a clearing in the middle, a protected retreat. John Muir once wrote of a similar experience: "I made my bed in a nook of the pine thicket . . . snug as squirrel nests, well ventilated, full of spicy odors, and with plenty of wind-played needles to sing one asleep."

In the morning we walked to Pear Lake before pausing for one of the most delightful breakfasts of the trip: our quart of fresh huckleberries served liberally over granola and drenched with honey and milk.

Just east of Cady Pass, a damp meadow provided a spongy bed that night. The temperature dropped drastically, and we awoke under a powdering of frost. Each blade of grass, each leaf and pine needle was etched with delicate crystals of ice.

But by the time we reached Lake Sally Ann, the sun had chased away most of the cold, and we rolled out our bags to dry. Across the lake, half a dozen hoary marmots were sunning themselves on a rockslide; they eyed us nervously at first, then gradually settled down. A few minutes later we heard a chorus of their shrill whistles and watched as they abruptly disappeared among the rocks. Then I spotted the reason: A large red-tailed hawk glided past, only 20 feet above the rocks. When it had coasted away, the marmots gradually reappeared, whistling at first tentatively and then defiantly.

An up-and-down segment of trail marked by meadows, tiny ponds, and sparkling springs brought us to White Pass in Glacier Peak Wilderness. Approaching the pass, I noticed a distant orange spot against a green hillside, and I was delighted when it turned out to be the down vest of roving wilderness ranger Ben Englebright, my climbing partner on Mount Rainier.

Ben's dominant trait is a rapturous response to wilderness, and particularly to the country around Glacier Peak. For 32 years he worked for an oil company, but throughout that time, he told me, "my real love was always mountain climbing and backpacking. Finally I decided to retire from the company and do what I wanted full time. The job gets better every year."

We set up camp near Ben's tent on a hillock protected from a powerful wind by a screen of fir trees. After supper, Ben joined us. "My wife and I had our first date here at White Pass." he reminisced. "We hiked up to watch the sunset—it was honestly the most beautiful I've ever seen."

Now Lois is a wilderness ranger, too, and she travels with Ben most of the time. That month she was filling in for the ranger at Kennedy Hot Springs.

Scudding gray clouds from the west promised rain, Ben told us the next morning; but it held off until afternoon. From White Pass the trail angles up a long alpine meadow to Red Pass. When we met hikers, Ben asked to see their wilderness permits, answered their questions, and explained various rules.

"Educating people to use the wilderness properly is the biggest part of my job," he said. "And I'm hopeful; I think people are learning. Every year, for example, there's less garbage and litter." After a pause he added, "In a sense I protect people from wilderness and the wilderness from people."

The valley of the White Chuck River, overshadowed by ice-clad, 10,568-foot Glacier Peak, engulfed us as we descended from Red Pass. On a faraway hill I spotted a tiny white blotch, and asked Ben hopefully whether it was a mountain goat. We watched for a while, and when the blotch didn't move, Ben kindly suggested that it could be either a rock or a tired goat resting. That was all the encouragement I needed. The more I thought about it, the more I convinced myself that the object was a mountain goat — the first I'd seen.

Ben left us to check some other camps, and we continued to Sitkum Creek, where the two-mile side trail to Kennedy Hot Springs cuts off the Pacific Crest Trail. The first raindrops that Ben had predicted began to fall, and soon a heavy drizzle was beating a tattoo on our rain gear.

A nearly deserted clearing bordered by the glacial flows of Kennedy Creek and the White Chuck River marked the Kennedy Hot Springs campground. When we had set up our tents, we walked over to the ranger's cabin and into the warm hospitality of Lois Englebright. She promptly prepared rose hip tea, imported from Europe and the gift of a Czech-Canadian couple whom Ben and Lois had helped. As we relaxed in the cozy, 50-year-old cabin, Sam asked Lois about the hot springs.

"One of them bubbles up into a walled pool," she explained. "You're lucky you're here now — midweek in late September. On nice summer weekends, people have to line up just to hop in the water for a few minutes."

Rain was dripping steadily on the tent when I awoke next morning. No one else was around. I decided my companions must be visiting Lois, so I set off to see the spring, expecting to find it empty. Instead, bobbing gently in the water, the picture of contentment, were Sam, Doug, and Ellen.

The pool, evidence of Glacier Peak's dormant volcanism, is about seven feet square and five feet deep. I promptly joined the rest and was washed by brown, effervescent water that varies only slightly from a delightful 98° F. After an hour's soak, we climbed out and packed our gear to leave. Then Sam suggested we take one final dip in the spring, and we ended up staying the whole rainy, cold afternoon. We even developed enough courage to run down to the White Chuck River and plunge into its frigid waters, then dashed back to the warmth of the spring.

Early the next morning we finally left — still in the rain. As the day passed I caught an occasional glimpse of the lower ribs of Glacier Peak when the clouds parted; a few hundred feet above, the rain was snow, turning the mountain walls white, but beneath my feet the earth was sodden and spongy. At Fire Creek Pass, 6,300 feet high, I walked briefly through the clouds.

A massive ice floe choked circular Mica Lake a mile below the pass. Near dusk I reached Milk Creek and began searching for a protected camping place to escape the now pouring rain. A quarter mile downstream on a side trail I found the ideal shelter — a natural cave formed by an overhanging cliff.

By the time Doug, Sam, and Ellen arrived, I had a fire started and was drying my boots and clothes.

Thirty-eight long, wet switchbacks led us to a ridge above Milk Creek, through a high valley cut by several springs, and down Vista Creek. Before we reached the Suiattle River, we walked through a damp wood where the diversity of funguses amazed me. Toadstools of many colors popped from the ground; broad-ribbed fans grew from tree trunks; black warty mushrooms crept from under fallen logs. I was especially intrigued by the half-dozen "mushroom cities" that I found: As many as 75 tiny beige plants clustered together in clumps a foot or two in width, like so many look-alike houses in a suburban development.

Miners Creek Shelter, a three-sided lean-to near the Suiattle River, housed us that night although we had to place our sleeping bags carefully to avoid several leaks in the roof. Beyond Miners Creek the trail skirts timberline on long Miners Ridge, site of a reserve of low-grade copper ore, and in a meadow we came on a camp left by an exploratory drilling crew. Under a provision of the Wilderness Act, mining claims established in wilderness preserves before 1984 can be worked; Kennecott Copper Company holds 17 patented claims on Miners Ridge.

When I wondered aloud if they would ever be developed, Mel Suchy, a mining engineer for the Forest Service, told me, "It's inevitable. The United States is now importing copper whereas just a few years ago, we were exporting. Someday the country will need that copper on Miners Ridge."

Two mining methods are feasible here. In the block caving method, miners would tunnel into the ridge, undercut the ore body, and permit it to collapse; the copper ore could then be removed through tunnels. The alternative would be to excavate an open pit two thousand feet in diameter and a thousand feet deep. Either method is certain to scar the land.

I walked around the deserted mining camp; the only sounds were the steady rainfall and the squishing of my boots in the mud. My eyes followed the uneven line of Miners Ridge, then dropped to the tree-lined valley of Miners Creek. A gentle gray mist rose from the valley floor; when it reached me with its transient veil, I turned my back on the camp and sadly walked on.

From Suiattle Pass we followed the forested gorge of Agnes Creek to the Stehekin River, at the junction of the boundaries of Glacier Peak Wilderness, North Cascades National Park, and Lake Chelan National Recreation Area. At the nearby community of Stehekin on Lake Chelan, we checked into North Cascades Lodge and escaped the cold rain for the first time in a week.

A shower, a hot meal, a good bed, and some dry clothes put the world into better perspective. With remarkable detachment I watched the rain speckle Chelan, a long, fiord-like lake bounded by towering cliffs.

In the lobby I met a couple who had hiked in Washington 35 years before I was born. "The first time we hiked together was in 1911," diminutive, 88-year-old Hazel Bennett told me. "We went from Mount Rainier to Mount Adams with a group of 35 people from Seattle." Her husband, Burt, tan and fit at 95, puffed on his pipe and listened attentively to our conversation, though he was obviously a gentleman of few words. He had taught political science at the University of Washington, and there he met Hazel, a school-teacher from Iowa.

"On October 1, 1915, we were married," Hazel continued, "and we spent our honeymoon retracing that hike of 1911. We had 17 days of the most beautiful weather, and the only people we saw were two Indians on horseback. After that, we took several more trips with large groups. And, you know, the friendships we made on those trips have lasted all these years." She patted her husband's hand, and he nodded. "We have some fine memories, some very fine memories."

Predictions that the rain would turn into heavy snow caused us to alter plans and leapfrog to Hart's Pass, 32 miles from the Canadian border. From the west side of Slate Peak we had a panoramic view: Steep-walled Ninety-nine Basin opened before us, and beyond stood ridge after ridge of the white-topped North Cascades. Impending winter confronted us in a cold, moisture-laden wind, and pewter skies foretold a season of snow.

Behind Slate Peak curls bowl-shaped Benson Basin. Above its ground cover of flaxen sedge grew the most surprising trees I have yet seen. The Lyall, or subalpine, larch is a distinctive conifer; in the fall its short needles turn amber and, when fired by the setting sun, shimmer like molten gold. Among the somber greens of hemlocks, pines, and firs, a larch grove stands out like a peacock among starlings.

At Windy Pass we crossed into Pasayten Wilderness and on Tamarack Peak looked north to Canada, trying to visualize the trace of the border.

A small stand of pines provided a camping place at Goat Lakes Basin. Sitting by the fire, I heard a sound like the stamping of boots. At first I thought it was my imagination, but it happened again. Walking toward the trees, Doug and I heard the sound still again, but found nothing in the beams of our

"Waiting for the others, I started a fire and dried my boots and clothes."

flashlights. We returned to the fire, puzzled and wary. Suddenly the sound resumed just a few feet behind me; I whirled and snapped on my flashlight. Two yellow eyes gleamed in the light; then, as I shifted the beam, I made out a graceful tawny doe.

A storm front marched across the sky at dawn and platoons of sullen gray clouds darkened the whole day. As we passed Three Fools Peak and climbed to windswept Lakeview Ridge, I decided that winter had finally snuffed the final breath of fall.

On the shore of Hopkins Lake we made our last camp. A fire combated the cold for a couple of hours; then we climbed into our sleeping bags. But I lay open-eyed for hours, watching clouds play across the constellations, listening to a tree creaking in the wind, wondering if it would fall that night.

My thoughts went back over our long journey, and I felt again the joy of walking through the land, observing, contemplating, marveling. I remembered the hour-to-hour changes in terrain, the day-to-day changes in weather, the week-to-week changes in season—and even more gradual changes in myself. Along the way I had learned to set aside some of the habits of my city life and to heed the advice of Ralph Waldo Emerson: "Adopt the pace of nature. Her secret is patience."

The October dawn came early—and cold. My thermometer registered 20°, and there was a layer of ice on a container of water we had left out.

Only seven miles now separated us from the Canadian border, and we walked fast to stay warm—but not too fast to talk. I told Sam some of my thoughts of the previous night, and he said, "After walking on this trail for so long, I feel as if it's kind of a telegraph line—as if we're still connected in some way to every point along the trail, and to every person we've met on it."

Two more switchbacks brought us into a small clearing, and in the center I spotted a bronze obelisk: Monument 78—the end of the trail—seven miles from the Trans-Canada Highway. Sam and I took off our packs, leaned them against the monument, and shook hands across the international boundary. When Doug and Ellen appeared a few minutes later we congratulated them with equal fanfare. Then we celebrated with a packet of freeze-dried shrimp cocktail that I had been carrying for just this occasion.

As I shouldered my pack, I thought of something John Muir wrote near the end of his life: "Plants, animals, birds, rocks, gardens, magnificent clouds, thunderstorms, rain, hail—all, all have blessed me!"

I glanced southward down the trail for the last time. In my mind I could see all the way to a barbed wire fence strung across the desert.

Veteran hikers Hildur and Franklin Blocksom pause at a switchback turn near Lake Susan Jane. "We climb in September to collect berries for canning," explains Franklin, 76, "and to enjoy the trail when it's not crowded."

ABOVE: A MUSHROOM CITY

Plump huckleberries, picked from bushes turning scarlet in autumn, reward Ellen Smith during a rest break. A brilliant mixture of low shrubs colors the North Cascades mountainside, signaling the change of seasons.

*"We picked fat, ripe huckleberries
until we had filled a quart pot
as well as our stomachs."*

Icy waters of the White Chuck River, fed by thaws on Glacier Peak, spill around mossy rocks near a cabin used by wilderness rangers Lois and Ben Englebright. Only a few yards away, Doug, Ellen, and Will soak in the bubbling, 98° pool of Kennedy Hot Springs. "The thermal spring's a leftover from Glacier Peak's volcanic origins," observes Ben. "Every summer a couple of thousand backpackers stop here to take a warm dip."

Dark storm cloud sweeps toward jagged peaks of Washington's North Cascades, threatening more September snow. From this 6,350-foot elevation at Fire Creek Pass, the trail zigzags down the ridge past lakes icebound throughout the year. Sudden, severe storms make trail conditions in the Cascades "subject to change without notice." Opposite, frosted huckleberry leaves warn of winter's early arrival in America's Alps.

Elk cows spar in the midst of a herd wintering in the Cascade foothills of Washington. Driven from higher elevations by snow, the elk linger here until the weather warms in spring. Then, in small bands, they gradually migrate back into the mountains of Snoqualmie National Forest, following the greening grasses. Occasionally seen by hikers along the trail, they inhabit timbered areas near meadows where they can graze.

*Striding down Devils Stairway, Doug swings his arms in exuberance
as he nears the Canadian border. At journey's end, Sam and Will toast
the 2,400-mile Pacific Crest Trail and the friends met during their
trek. Behind them, Monument 78 marks the northern end of the trail.
"We hiked more than seven months to reach that goal," Will recalled.
"When we got there we felt physically spent but emotionally fulfilled."*

*"We felt we were still
connected in some way
with every point
along the trail."*

DOUG GOSLING

195

IN HARMONY
WITH WILDERNESS
AN EPILOGUE

THE WILDERNESS PRESERVES of America are, or ought to be, realms "where the earth and its community of life are untrammeled by man, where man himself is a visitor who does not remain." That conviction, expressed in the Wilderness Act, has helped to generate a new vision of wilderness use based not on the needs and desires of man but on the protection and preservation of land, water, air, plants, and animals.

The governing ethic holds that people should exist in harmony with their natural surroundings whether on a Sunday picnic in a city park or on a long-distance hike along the Pacific Crest Trail. The basic tenet is a simple one: Leave no trace of your passing.

Certain guidelines are helpful. Where possible, avoid camping within a hundred feet of a lake or stream. Try to choose a bare spot or rocky area where living plants will not be crushed. Scrupulously avoid polluting any body of water: Wash dishes away from streams, use only biodegradable soap —if you must use any at all—and bury human waste far from water, trail, and campsite. Carry out all litter; I reserved one pocket in my pack for trash. And scatter the rocks of any windbreak or fire ring that you build.

Wood campfires, although pleasant, are rarely necessary; cook on a lightweight backpacking stove. If you do build a fire, keep it small and burn only downed branches and twigs. Never chop or break limbs off living trees or shrubs, and when collecting fuel, leave the gnarled, silvery trunks of dead trees for their scenic beauty. Although both Sam and I enjoyed a fire and occasionally found one essential for drying out or warming up, we also discovered that it could be limiting. "A fire funnels your thoughts into it," Sam observed after our first few days of hiking, "and makes you miss a hundred other things like the display of stars and the sounds of the woods at night."

If you are interested in hiking part of the Pacific Crest Trail, a good starting point for information is the Pacific Crest Club, a nonprofit organization that publishes a quarterly journal. Membership applications can be obtained from Warren L. Rogers, Camp Research Foundation, Box 1907, Santa Ana, Calif. 92702.

The Wilderness Press of Berkeley, California, has published an excellent two-volume guide to the trail. For a listing of other books, see page 198.

Write directly to individual national forests and national parks for maps and up-to-date trail information. Topographic maps for the entire route are available from the Distribution Center, U. S. Geological Survey, Federal Center, Denver, Colo. 80225. The USGS supplies a free index to its maps.

Whether your experience with the Pacific Crest Trail is a weekend hike, a summer-long trek, or simply an evening or two spent reading this book, I hope your time will be as rewarding and fulfilling as mine has been. "Wherever we go in the mountains," mused John Muir, "we find more than we seek."

INDEX

Acknowledgments

The Special Publications Division is grateful to the individuals, organizations, and agencies named or quoted in the text and to those cited here for their generous cooperation and assistance during the preparation of this book: Lee Corbin, Roxanna Ferris, Gerald W. Gause, James W. Hughes, Ed Waldapfel, and Thomas Winnett; the U. S. Forest Service, the National Park Service, the California State Parks and Recreation Department, and the Smithsonian Institution.

Additional Reading

Clinton C. Clarke, *The Pacific Crest Trailway*; Francis P. Farquhar, *History of the Sierra Nevada*; Colin Fletcher, *The Complete Walker*; Harvey Manning, *Backpacking: One Step at a Time*; John Muir, *The Mountains of California* and *Our National Parks*; Jeff Schaffer and Bev and Fred Hartline, *The Pacific Crest Trail, Volume 2: Oregon and Washington*; Tracy I. Storer and Robert L. Usinger, *Natural History of the Sierra Nevada*; Thomas Winnett, *The Pacific Crest Trail, Volume 1: California*. National Geographic books: *Wilderness U.S.A.*; Ronald M. Fisher, *The Appalachian Trail*. In NATIONAL GEOGRAPHIC: Harvey Arden, "John Muir's Wild America," April 1973; Mike W. Edwards, "Mexico to Canada on the Pacific Crest Trail," June 1971; Nathaniel T. Kenney, "The Other Yosemite," June 1974, and "The Spectacular North Cascades," May 1968; and Robert Laxalt, "Golden Ghosts of the Lost Sierra," June 1974. Readers may also want to consult the National Geographic Index for related material.

Library of Congress CIP Data

Gray, William R. 1946-
The Pacific Crest Trail.

1. Pacific Crest Trail. 2. Hiking—Pacific States. 3. Pacific States—Description and travel—1951-   4. Gray, William R., 1946-   I. National Geographic Society, Washington, D. C. Special Publications Division. II. Title.
F851.G8   917.9'04'3   74-1565
ISBN 0-87044-149-3

Composition for *The Pacific Crest Trail* by National Geographic's Phototypographic Division, Carl M. Shrader, Chief; Lawrence F. Ludwig, Assistant Chief. Printed and bound by Fawcett Printing Corp., Rockville, Md. Color separations by Chanticleer Press, Inc., New York, N.Y.; Graphic Color Plate, Inc., Stamford, Conn.; Progressive Color Corp., Rockville, Md.; and J. Wm. Reed Co., Alexandria, Va.